ADVANCE PRAISE FOR
HOW CAN WE MAKE YOUR POWER MORE COMFORTABLE

"An alchemist of language, Ball's gumbo of puns, allusions and insider info brings the hysterical out of the historical….His approach to the essay is all hybrid vigor— the blood of the poet swirling in a journalist…with the chutzpah to speak satire to power."
—Kirpal Gordon, author, *Ghost & Ganga, A Jazz Odyssey*

"Often very funny, always incisive with insights that deflate the hot air of contemporary society and its inept leaders, Ball both entertains and alarms as he penetrates the follies of our time. His own skillful use of language exposes the semantic fabrications that prop up so many of our political and economic policies."
—Walter Cummins, Editor Emeritus, *The Literary Review*

"These essays display a vast range of interests and curiosity couched often in satire. Take one step beyond reality and you've wandered happily into Ball's delightfully erudite world."
—Hampden H. Smith III, Professor Emeritus, Department of Journalism and Mass Communications, Washington & Lee University

"Ball...mobilizes enormous and uncountable numbers of ideas, about virtually every aspect of our culture. When you read him, you aren't revisiting notions you already had; you're facing real challenges, sentence by unpredictable sentence. If you want to be enlivened, rather than lulled to sleep, you should read Norman Ball."

—Stephen Cox, Editor, *Liberty Magazine*

HOW CAN WE MAKE
YOUR POWER
MORE COMFORTABLE?

ESSAYS

*

HOW CAN WE MAKE YOUR POWER MORE COMFORTABLE?

ESSAYS

*

NORMAN BALL

—DEL SOL PRESS • WASHINGTON D. C.—

Copyright © 2010 Del Sol Press

DEL SOL PRESS, WASHINGTON, D. C.

Paper ISBN: 1-934832-12

First Edition

Cover photo by Luigi De Frenza from Biennale di Venezia 2005

Cover & Interior Design by Ander Monson

Publication by Del Sol Press/Web Del Sol Association, a not-for-profit corporation under section 501(c)(3) of the United States Internal Revenue Code.

CONTENTS

Acknowledgments   iii
Foreword   v
Introduction   1

— GUFFAWS —

How Can We Make Your Power More Comfortable?   7
The Meek Shall Inherit Mounting Legal Bills   9
Who's Counting the Counters?   11
The Night Candidate Smith's Rubber Chicken Was Spiked with Sodium Pentothal   14
The Home is the Temple of the Dole   16
He Who Controls the Search Controls the Future   19
The Stalls of Power: Don't Tap, Don't Tell   22
It Takes One Child to Raze a Village   25
The Global Conspiracy against Shit Just Happening   29
The Puppet Masters of Ball   31
Quayle Hunting   35
Read Our Lips   37
Lay Down, Kenny   39
The Big Easy Heads East   41
Thirty-Year Pin   43

Probing the Outer Limits of Intergalactic Probity (or, "Take Me to Your Feeder Fund")   46

— POLITICAL ANIMALS —

Battle Hymn of a Republic   53
Sez Me   62
When You Wish Upon a Czar   66
Now We See You, Now We Vote   69
The Privileged Few and the Budgeted Many   76
All the World's a Phase   81
One Nation, Under Whose God?   86
Big Government and the Big Easy   91
The Bush Whacking the Dog   100
On the Recent Free Speech Flap, Imus Confess My Reservations   103
Mr. Prime Minister?   108
Back to the Future with Guernica: The Sentimental Impulse and the Fundamentalist Appeal   116
Why a White Man Shouting 'Race!' Always Makes a Shrill Sound in a Crowded Theatre   120
In a Global Village, No One Can Hear You Scream   129
Nothing but Nihilism   133
Gathering The Herd   139
Hoisting Yank Petard with Baudrillard   142
A Barrel of Verse Is Like Monkeys in the Bank   147
Fanning the Embers of Localism: The Late Great Broadcast Affiliate System   151

— WAR FOOTING —

Absence Makes the Hawk Grow Stronger   161
War Stories   166
Hubris and Its Perennial Nemesis, War   174
Suspicious White Powder: Bad Actors in an Age of Bad Equality   177

Flames of Our Fathers   182
The Manifest Hijacking of Destiny   186

— CURRENCY OF THE REALM —

The Mill-Race: Overproduction, Interrupted   195
It's Our Money and We'll Lie if We Want To   201
When Currency Becomes a Fiat for Oxygen, All Breathing Must
    Leave the Room   208
Dining on the Future: An Inward-Out Exploration of Cosmic
    Retribution, Alienation and Market Dynamics   215
Sometimes, It Really Is Different This Time   220
Metropolis, Ezra Pound, Mammon and the Law of Too-Large
    Numbers   225

ACKNOWLEDGMENTS

I'd like to thank the many journal and magazine editors who carried a number of these essays previously in their publications. Those venues include *Main Street Rag, The Potomac: A Journal of Poetry and Politics, Liberty, Generation X National Journal, Hazmat Literary Review, Mobius: The Journal of Social Change, November 3rd Club Journal, Clamor, Identity Theory, Wolf Moon Journal, Eclectica, Burst!, Epicenter, Del Sol Review, Free DTV Plus, Unlikely Stories, Bright Lights Film Journal, Noo Journal, iTulip, Ambush Arts* and *The Anthony Burgess Foundation Journal*.

I'd also like to thank the many folks who have lent me their ears and in many cases no small amount of work rendering this jumble of essays into a coherent whole. Those people include Gene Justice, Todd Peterson, Leo Girard, Jeff Crouch and of course editor Mike Neff. Also to my girlfriend Kimberly and son Gregory, I thank you for showing more patience than I deserved as my eyes were so often glued to the computer screen, my writer's notebook. Finally, to my late, great friend Douglas Milton whose infectious enthusiasm is on abundant display in the foreword to this book.

FOREWORD
BY
DOUGLAS MILTON

In his excellent autobiography the late left-wing journalist and novelist Claud Cockburn tells of a political cartoonist in the 1930's whose drawings were once known and feared by the mighty for their savagery. Suddenly he stopped producing, and a concerned friend, encountering him in the street, asked why. The reason was simple. Current events had become so grotesque that there was no longer any need for caricature. 'These days', said the erstwhile cartoonist ruefully, 'photography suffices'. Or as Juvenal put it, 'It's hard NOT to write satire'.

Cockburn is little read these days for the simple reason that his work is out of print, but his autobiography *I, Claud* (soon to be reissued by *CounterPunch*) should be required reading for anyone contemplating a career in political journalism, especially in the United States. Cockburn spent much of the 1920's as New York and Washington correspondent for the *London Times*, and had no problem reconciling Communist convictions with a deep love of America that was to last all his life.

His sons Alexander, Andrew and Patrick have carried on the good work—or the relentless bleeding-heart liberal chipping away at all that's good and pure and true and Republican in God's own country, depending on your point of view. And if you incline to the latter, it probably makes it worse that these nit-picking no-goodniks aren't even American. Any more than is that egregious Englishman Christopher Hitchens, whose status as the US's National Gadfly has now eclipsed even that of the ornery but impeccably American Gore Vidal, who once silkily pronounced Hitchens to be his dauphin. Until recently, Vidal prudently chose exile in Italy from whence to launch his poisoned darts, whereas Hitchens and the Cockburn brothers made straight for Washington and the jugular.

One can see a tradition taking shape here; young, British, passionately left-wing journalists taking up cudgels on behalf of an America about which they're equally passionate. It's an appealing picture, illustrative of the French copybook maxim *'Qui aime bien, châtie bien'*. But it's perhaps a little too neat. For one thing, that particular generation of ex-pat mudslingers is no longer young. To say that they have become Establishment would be absurd and insulting. Hitchens in particular has refused to be pigeonholed as a standard lefty with all the expected and acceptable *partis-pris*. His book on Clinton, *No One Left To Lie To*, sent shockwaves through Democratic party circles, and was the cause of not a few broken friendships (including, spectacularly, with Alexander Cockburn), and for many of his admirers his stance on the Iraq war—pro, despite his obvious contempt for the Bush administration—is baffling and dismaying in equal measure.

And as if that weren't enough, with his latest book *God Is Not Great*, he cheerfully takes on all the major world religions, despite frequent death threats to him and his family from those who love God so much that, darn it, they just can't help but want to kill some folks to prove it. So, one can spend several decades in the thick of US politics and still resist the temptation to settle into the expected role of Loveable Old Grouch.

Nevertheless, it's a poor lookout for polemical journalism if a new generation isn't already firing up its laptops—a lame substitute for 'champing at the bit' I know, but the subject of this introduction tolerates clichés like the Taliban tolerate lesbian moms—finding its own voice, and offering its own perspectives on the weird and wonderful proto-fascist landscape of Palin Americana. Might it be time for the Old Gang to get the hell out of the way?

Which brings us to Norman Ball. A couple of years ago I was asked to guest-edit an issue of *The End of the World News*, a biannual magazine put out by the International Anthony Burgess Foundation in Manchester. I was a novice editor, but I was lucky. The standard of the contributions was high. I already knew most of the writers from prior Burgess conferences and I'd specifically asked them for pieces because, on past form, whatever was submitted was bound to be erudite, witty and above all original. However one essay came as a bolt from, as it were, the Red, White and Blue. Entitled *All the World's a Phase* (and included herein), it distinguished itself immediately from all other submissions by being not about literature or music so much as politics, and US politics at that, a subject upon which Burgess had only touched from time to time in the context of a book review or the US sections of his autobiography.

But here was this newcomer, Norman Ball, taking Burgess's early sci-fi-theology novel *The Wanting Seed* and using its argument—that political systems seem to veer between stern Augustinianism and wishy-washy Pelagianism, as a sort of grid through which to examine, with caustic wit, the current State of the Union and more specifically the state of things in the ongoing security-versus-liberty debate that so dominates the current American political scene. The piece attracted a lot of intrigued comment, as well as the obvious question,'Who's Norman Ball?'

Well, as I now know, the man whose multifarious and nefarious works you are about to read is an intriguing poet, an erudite literary essayist, a satirical political commentator and an accomplished singer-songwriter to boot. Although I've dealt largely with Norman's polemic broadsides, his poetry, reminiscent at its best of Pope, sneaks in at opportune times to bring some iambic grace to the scrum.

In addition to his other virtues, Norman Ball is a Scot, transplanted to a home in Virginia from which he can glower across the Potomac at the Washington Monument as he broods on just what the dedicatee would have made of the way we live now. I'm a Scot too, living in Paris, and it's to Norman that I owe, after a few years of virtually daily transatlantic emails, such increased understanding of US politics, politicians and sheer barefaced chicanery as I now possess.

And you know what? He makes it funny—appallingly, gut-bustingly, beer-coming-out-your-nose funny. For a start, he has the best way with a title since Hunter S. Thompson (see contents page). Time after time, receiving the latest barbed missive slipped under the tent-flaps of Homeland Insecurity, I'd find myself abandoning all hope of work for the next hour as I read, reread and then forwarded the article to those like-minded souls out there once described by Auden as 'ironic points of light'. Likeminded but not necessarily alike politically, Norman Ball has fans from way across the political spectrum, the sort of alert, humorous intelligent open-minded people who enjoy a good knock-down argument, who wouldn't dream of being so arrogant as to claim a monopoly on truth; the sort of people in fact, who are fast becoming an endangered species in an America which, in the post-911-gone-tea-bagger environment, has become so traumatized that it is in danger of accepting any remedy, any medicine however nasty the taste, if only it will take the bad dreams go away.

Ball strikes me as being the best of a very select band of younger political writers fit to wrest the baton and run with it. And it's startling to think that, taking the long view, he's only just started. Just how finely will he have honed his *saeva indignatio* in ten years' time? The 21st century heirs of Ozymandias would really, really like to know.

Nabokov (himself no slouch when it came to dissecting wily wasps posing as benevolent butterflies) once referred in passing to his 'dream-bright America'. After a fast-receding beatific interlude with Obama, the dreams are resuming their nightmarish cast and too many Americans seem prepared to trade the freedoms that are their birthright for a one-way ticket to a bright new dawn—however illusory that may turn out to be.

Well, the writer of the essays and poems in this book can't promise you, the reader, any such thing. For the calming bedtime story, the televangelist's soothing smile, the reassuring hiss of balloon juice, apply elsewhere. But in his political journalism, his poetry, his literary reflections and in the occasional piece of sheer black farce, Norman Ball can at least help you distinguish the bad dreams, and our leaders' mad dreams, from the not altogether hopeless reality.

INTRODUCTION

This compendium is a diary capturing much of what has intrigued me in a political vein over the last three or four years. A mordant tone twists the knife best. That's my motto anyway. Seeing it all packed together, I'm struck also by the stubborn repetition of certain themes, evidence no doubt of a compulsive mind.

War was a bedeviling preoccupation. We pushed on strings, hoping to hoist flags. No definitive hero ever arrived. Brave and noble young men and women died for reasons that continue to resist concise explanation. It's as though Osama bin Laden conjured a Rorschach-stained field of engagement upon which we, with military imprecision, enacted every possible nightmare. Despite a fearsome array of 21st century weaponry, our every move seemed to launch from an odd reactivity—or was it a well-armed passivity? Perhaps ambivalence, the so-called fog of war, will be the hallmark of all future conflicts.

My sense is that coherence has unraveled from the top down. The chastened heartland will never offer up such unabashed *esprit de corps* again. The salt of the earth is getting hip to the Halliburton beat (the latter freshly ensconced in Dubai like a well-heeled carpetbagger.) Reflexive patriotism, certainly its more jingoist manifestation, can be something akin to the greater fool theory, particularly in the hands of a nefarious ruling class.

One imagines David Halberstam's ghost lamenting some narrative stone left unturned: Had we better explicated the Vietnam debacle, Iraq would never have happened. When it's not selling us out, language is still the best weapon for coaxing meaning from morass. People need stories with their guns and butter.

Perhaps tiring of war, the collapsing narrative then trained its incoherence on the economy. Whatever one's ideological persuasion, it's hard to dispute that four hundred years of banker-led capitalism created the modern world. However nothing adds up anymore. How then will the growth imperative of modern capitalism address issues of sustainability or the finitude of resources?

Good manners demand leavening despair with hope. Here then is my bromidic contribution: While the world goes to hell in a hand basket, if we all pull together we can avert catastrophe. There. How's that for Live Earth - We Are the World put-your-back-into-it-ness punctuated with a really kick-ass global concert? Pass the torch to a proper rock god who'll take our better angels to the bridge. Even among the most cynical there is a wish to be attentive audience. We're trained for resolutions, the tidier the better.

There is an alchemical notion—buttressed it seems by recent quantum cosmology—that from the darkest dark, light emerges. Cosmologists have suggested we inhabit a universe optimally configured for black hole production while life is the occasional industrial accident on the factory floor. Even the Book of Genesis, that great polemic on man's stewardship of all things, concedes the *a priori* status of darkness. Then there's the fitting homily: 'it's always darkest before the light'. Dark matter's universal primacy is eerily anticipated throughout the metaphysical record.

And yet, there's no great pleasure in being mere adjuncts of happenstance. So we forge ahead unbowed by our receding centrality. Only we can prevent forest fires. Mothball that SUV. The term itself—global warming—smacks of parochialism as the Martian poles melt with equal dispatch. Apparently the great Copernican project—aimed at prying us from the-center-of-things—is a perpetual revolution prone to setback. Further confounding Al Gore's global crusade, Pluto, Jupiter and Triton are warming too. Alas had Al only stopped at inventing the Internet.

I have a theory. Faced with phenomena beyond our reach and ken and in a bid to match the tenor of the present cosmic flux, human conflicts escalate sympathetically. Nihilism is humanity's devised response (what paradox) to the oncoming Mother Void. Indeed our looming fate feels larger than humanity itself, determinable by the stars, certainly by our own star. Fear compels us to stalk a familiar horse, ourselves. There is no fitting cultural response should the Sun elect an absent burp or hiccup. Purveyors and pariahs alike of the Western canon will perish together.

In the life-hostile, radiation-filled vacuum that is this universe (predominantly), tiny enclaves of conscious life may well manifest a foreboding sense when their own peril draws near. We are so unfathomably improbable, so miraculous (in the non-religious sense, if you please), that when the darkness returns to reassert its hegemony, we will be faintly, achingly aware of its imminent approach. We make noise to drown out a larger noise, our inevitable cessation. Here then is a small contribution to the cacophony.

GUFFAWS

HOW CAN WE
MAKE YOUR POWER
MORE COMFORTABLE?

Bowing to the pressures of modern politics, the Nation's Business decided to resign effective immediately and throw its weight behind a perpetual, unremitting election cycle.

Speaking on behalf of the Nation's Business, Uncle Sam acknowledged that political capital was being squandered needlessly on issues of substance leaving huge wellsprings of pandering in the lurch. The nation, said Sam, was looking forward to the endless diversion offered by self-congratulatory confetti blizzards, ticker tape parades and glitzy ballroom galas.

Said Sam: "The next two years have been deemed a 'lame duck period' both by power-seekers and the folks that watch them. Everyone knows nothing of consequence occurs in a lame duck period. The Nation's Business has thus decided to abandon the pressing nature of its concerns which were becoming a real source of irritation in some political circles."

In a rare joint communiqué, the DNC and RNC chairmen welcomed the move, saying: "We applaud the nation's efforts not to hog the spotlight so that the real business of America, jockeying for power, can consume the remaining two years of the current four year term." Joining the chorus of support was The Eighth Graders of America League (EGAL) which estimates 5% of its membership has already formed exploratory committees for the 2038 presidential campaign. In the words of one pimply pre-teen, it's never too early to test the political waters, especially during study hall.

Adding to the general sense of inertia is the looming mid-term election cycle when all things come to a grinding halt, having just acquired a modicum of speed from the prior grinding halt brought upon, quite understandably, by the presidential election cycle.

One constitutional scholar suggested that future governance in America might resemble hunting season for the Eastern Bobcat, that is, a brief sixty-day window occurring twice each decade. Much however would depend on the resident squirrel population and whether the Bobcat lobby could mount a successful filibuster.

Confirming the trend toward electo-centric governance, TIME On-line Edition (March 12, 2006) reports (would a satirist kid you?) that looming nuclear confrontation with Iran may 'help [Bush's] numbers a little bit', thus taking some of the limp out of his lame and proving that even mushroom clouds have silver linings, birth defects notwithstanding.

Indeed global incineration is being hailed in some quarters as just what the doctor ordered to get serious governance back on its feet. The political class is not so ebullient however. Said one Washington infighter who moonlights as a lobbyist for hostile foreign interests: "The question is not whether American governance is best left to the whim and caprice of a handful of crazy imams. The question is how will pre-election straw polls be conducted in a post-apocalyptic landscape?

Only time—and a succession of Gallup polls—will tell.

THE MEEK SHALL INHERIT MOUNTING LEGAL BILLS

"Members of the Christian Music Trade Association (CMTA), an organization which specifically represents the interests of record companies, last week sent official resolutions to Congress asking for support in recognizing the importance of protecting music transmitted over digital broadcast radio from piracy."—March 20, 2006 (as reported on <www.breathecast.com>).

The latest sectarian discord spilled over into the music industry recently when the Christian Music Trade Association (CMTA) fired a salvo at the generally unarmed and God-fearing pirates of gospel music. The dilemma is this: gospel music, traditionally the province of divine inspiration, is being proliferated at a rate not seen since Jesus' replication of bread and fish during his widely bootlegged Sermon on the Mount. Thus, while the ranks of the believers are swelling, the industry itself is losing billions every year. The good news is that the Good News is getting out. Alas, the collection plate is none the richer for the revived interest.

Said an unrepentant CMTA spokesman: "The fact is evangelists got a free ride for centuries. It's just that, up until now, no one pressed the copyright issue. The IPod is forcing us to take a harder look."

Meanwhile that grand dame of the religion business, the Vatican, was quick to counter the CMTA's assertions, arguing that, on the contrary, free access to religious music has a market-enlarging effect. Said a Vatican spokesman: "Over the millennia, it's been the Holy Roman Church's contention that tithing increases when believers are left to sing for their suppers unharassed. So we never pressed the issue." Actually, this is not entirely accurate as, in 467, Pope Odious XIV attempted an 'alms for psalms' program only to be run out of town into the arms of restless Visigoth hordes who preferred bluegrass.

Still, there can be no doubt the CMTA isn't turning any cheeks: "Our industry group feels the time has come to crack down. The message is clear: wherever you rejoice in the Lord with unauthorized recorded music, we will hunt you down."

It's worth noting there are some reports, albeit in indecipherable ancient tongues, that God is still mulling His legal options. However judging by the alacrity of the avian flu mutations—not to mention the recent tidal wave of tsunamis—many heaven-watchers suspect serious biblical wrath just ahead. Indeed church sanctuaries are abuzz with rumors that God is contemplating, in the salty words of one clergyman, 'a really kick-ass flood that would bury all property disputes—indeed the whole of civilization—at the bottom of the sea.'

Reached between rehearsals for a re-match with Charlie Daniels, a fiddling Lucifer could only click his cloven hoofs and mutter, "This job's getting too damned easy."

Amen and out.

WHO'S COUNTING THE COUNTERS?

"Six U.S. census workers died in fatal car crashes in the last week in Texas, Florida, South Carolina and California, officials said."—UPI (May 4, 2010)

Reacting to a recent spate of census worker deaths, the Census Bureau has decided to sell its government vehicles, circle the wagons and extrapolate the nation's population from the Nielsen ratings for *The Real Housewives of Orange County*. As a last bureaucratic resort, the Bureau Chief has even considered bolting into Congress with a bag over his head screaming, "There's a helluva lot of us. Period. End of story."

But don't count on it.

As Census spokesman Ruff Talley points out, "Every dead counter is becoming a subtraction on the road to a full accounting. We could hire more census takers. But we run the risk of emptying the nation. And what's the point of completing a census if we're left with ghost towns and unattended lawns? We fear an *Omega Man* syndrome where the last guy standing will be a census taker with the acting chops of Charlton Heston. Even worse, he will have scads of government-issued number-two pencils and access to millions of abandoned vehicles."

Thus the idea for *National Wave Day* was hatched. From a conspicuous location, every American would be required by law to raise his right arm at 12 noon EST on August 14 for a period of fifteen minutes. The same military drones used to routinely incinerate unsuspecting Afghan villagers from high altitudes would crisscross the nation, performing the massive count.

One small-government advocate applauded the new proposal: "It's time for a rigorous self-inventorying in America anyway. Each citizen should be responsible for affirming his own numeric status. Who needs a costly network of pedestrian middlemen?" Some privacy advocates were more guarded. "Maybe I shave under my arms. Maybe I don't. How do I know my armpit data won't fall into the clutches of underhanded deodorant companies?"

However most households, already befuddled by the fractional headcount of the average American family (3.14) and its implications for the missing .86 person, are expressing a wistful nostalgia for the stranger with broken English asking incredibly personal questions on the nation's doorsteps. Said one lady: "Frankly I'm not comfortable standing on my front porch with my entire family waving to a nice drone in the sky. What if it's a plot to convert us all to Islam or worse, communism?

Even the amputee community is up in arms. "I lost my upper limbs in a thresher accident. But I'm a damned good American", said one. While his friend offered, "I may not be able to gesticulate wildly, but my heart's in the right place."

In an odd alliance at first thought to signal a coal-burning-plane initiative, the United Mine Workers joined the Airline Pilots Association in highlighting the inherent unfairness of a headcount protocol that favors people visible only on the ground. "We urge all Americans to protest this narrow proposal vigorously. The alternative-altitude community isn't going to take it anymore. ALPA spokesman Skye Bourne said, "We're up to here with sea-level chauvinism in its myriad forms." His UMW counterpart added, "Our friends in the ALPA can count on us. We're digging in beneath the grass-roots level for a long subterranean fight."

Eager to set a cooperative tone for the nation, President Obama attempted some arm-twisting of his own. "I don't need hands and arms to turn the pages of my interminable procession of speeches. I have a teleprompter. As long as I can gaze off into the distance with a concerned expression, you can count on me. My arm will be raised. Thus to those remaining Americans who have yet to tune out my voice, I say, wave for the nation. Our population requires your continued presence. For without you, we are Antarctica."

There's been no shortage of existential hand-wringing, especially within the professorial ranks. One fuzzy-headed academic whose Descartes has apparently long since run off with his horse, offered this: "I for one am one. You, on the other hand, furnish the existential predicament often postulated, provisionally, as two. Unless of course someone is reading over your shoulder in which case we make a cozy little threesome. Or do we? How can I be sure you're really there?"

The dilemma is hardly limited to the esoteric realms of academia. Indeed the question is as urgent as it is disarmingly plaintive: How can we count for something when our hands are so thoroughly tied?

        The Census Bureau hates to cause alarm.
        But your presence hinges squarely on your arm.

THE NIGHT CANDIDATE SMITH'S RUBBER CHICKEN WAS SPIKED WITH SODIUM PENTOTHAL

Good evening Ladies and Gentlemen.

First of all, let me say that you and the loved ones accompanying you here tonight look, on the whole, rather bedraggled and distracted, in marked contrast to the beaming family unit that stands behind me on this podium. Clearly my image means a lot to me. And it should. I have spent a lifetime simulating its rigorous demands.

I'd like to use this moment—and all who are here with me tonight—to register my vociferous opposition to family values in all their permutations. It's time we faced squarely the growing scourge of attaching value to those who are attached to us merely by marriage, blood or adoption. The nuclear family is a cancer eating at the heart of the body politic. I say, eat out America! We must rise up and expose families for the Rockwellian charade they are. America can do better! Should you support me in this cause, my devoted and comely legislative aide, Cindy Tandem, will be eternally in your debt. Cindy, why don't you stand up and wave to the crowd? Isn't she a looker, ladies and gentlemen?

Let me add that the Stepford wife and improbably happy teenagers who join me on this dais tonight owe their sunny dispositions largely to the wondrous effects of Valium and Ritalin, respectively. Yes, the pharmaceutical industry has been indispensable to this campaign, infusing my message with an eerie serenity that would not have been possible through organic means alone. So I attribute my success in no small measure to good, sound FDA-approved drugs. As for the citizenry of this land, well, your trust never ceases to amaze me. I would laugh but I've been trained by some of the best media advisors in the business to maintain a posture of unflappable dignity except on those occasions when I'm beating my wife.

In fact, it's my periodic bouts of spousal abuse that have left me rather ambivalent on the whole law and order thing. I swear there are some days you could tip me either way with a feather on that issue.

I am the first to concede that my dear wife Miriam is trapped in a loveless marriage. If truth be told—and strangely it seems to be this evening—my punishing schedule has rendered us virtual strangers for decades.

Some of you may have noticed that my second-oldest son, Josh, bears little resemblance either to myself or to his mother. However he is a dead ringer for my long-time friend and campaign manager, Richard Gotlieb. Richard, perhaps you could stand up and let everyone make their own informed decision. There he is, ladies and gentlemen! He's been giving me the off-message signal all evening. Hey Rich, get off my wife first, okay? Hah! Just kidding. He's doing a great job, ladies and gentlemen.

Vote for me this November and I promise I will do everything in my power to enlarge my power, addressing you at all times in an unctuous, patronizing manner. I will also strive to maintain the façade that your inconsequential dreams hold a snowball's chance in this roiling furnace of ambition we call politics!

God Help America and good night!

THE HOME IS THE TEMPLE OF THE DOLE

"The great jurist Sir Edward Coke, who lived from 1552 to 1634, has explained why the term mortgage comes from the Old French words mort, "dead," and gage, "pledge." It seemed to him that it had to do with the doubtfulness of whether or not the mortgagor will pay the debt."—from The American Heritage Dictionary etymology of 'mortgage'

In a bid to rescue upside-down homeowners from their mortgages, Uncle Sam is contemplating the single largest eminent domain land-grab since the Bolsheviks repoed the Czar's palaces. Called the Ponzi Omnibus Reconciliation & Killer Yard Sale Act, or PORKYS for short, this sweeping legislation is being hailed as the granddaddy of all sweetheart loans not to mention a last-ditch effort to save the American way of life. Under this scheme the Federal government will assume every mortgage in America thereby slashing the onerous debt burden of the vast majority of its beleaguered citizens. For their part, Americans will retain occupancy of their residences in order to take the trash out, watch *American Idol* and keep the porchlight on as a means to signaling someone is still home.

But first, what exactly derailed America's inexorable march towards capital punishment by homeowners' association tribunals? Suffice to say that, with the Oregon Trail paved over and the West largely won, the descendants of America's pioneers are mailing their keys back by the thousands. The word's out: rootlessness is the debt collector's worst nightmare, or as one indigent wag noted before fading into perpetual vagrancy, "best to keep moving."

If the housing bubble has taught us anything, it's that there's a dark side to unfettered accountability. In between trips to the suntan booth, the League of Permanently Sustainable and Inter-Denominational Ecstacy (LOPSIDE) president I. M. DeParte seemed to put his finger on all the lost fun: "Moral hazard poses the single gravest risk to our affluent lifestyle. Until people rise up against the homespun notion of paying bills, vacation homes are doomed. I call on all Good Time Charley's—before grabbing their golf clubs this morning—to contact their congressmen in support of this legislation. Today's sweat equity is tomorrow's child labor. We're well-rested and we're not going to take it anymore."

Others refuse to see the forest for the keys. Confusing Lockian principles for just another deadbolt manufacturer, one insolvent homeowner complained: "What's the point of private property if you can't get a home equity line of credit? Go ahead John, change the locks. I'm outta here."

Buried in the fine print of the Act is a $30 trillion 5-year ARM with 1 1/2 points which has the mortgage industry abuzz. Countryslide Travesty & Loan is hoping to get a slice of the business, and is elated at the prospect of having its 200,000 properties wiped off the books. "Frankly we were considering either thousands of suspiciously-set fires or an application for statehood," conceded Countryslide's eminently indictable CEO, Anthony 'Red' Flagg, as he toyed idly with one of those 7-Eleven bolt lighters. "So we're elated Uncle Sam recognized the public policy imperative of being the-dumbest-damned-lender-of-last-resort."

Always quick to scoop up easy money on behalf of his industry, Noam Hohm, President of the Associated Confab of Realtors Everywhere (ACRE) practically jumped out of his goofy yellow jacket with praise for the new legislation. "We're seeing a lot of things to like in residential socialism. First of all, there's no quibbling about commissions. Second, Uncle Sam could care less about the neighborhood as he'll soon own all of them anyway. An undiscerning buyer has always been our best customer. In this era of high fuel costs, it will reduce our members' drive-time, freeing them up for

THE HOME IS THE TEMPLE OF THE DOLE   17

the real business of cashing U.S. Treasury commission checks. This is a godsend."

Speaking of God, evangelicalism is proving no slouch in the underwriting business either. Should America lose either of its jobs as Moral Ombudsman to the World or Senior Purchaser of Crappy Chinese Products, The Big Guy Himself has promised to step in as Ultimate Bag-holder, at least according to the Right Reverend Pat Robertson, a man who wrestles regularly with competing voices in his head. Robertson does not paint a panacea however, conceding there is a 'deluge clause' wherein God can elect to flush the whole 'bricks and mortar thing' down the tubes should the payments become ungodly. "It's the best deal I could work out," confessed Robertson as he scrunched up his face like a constipated monkey simulating prayer. "But with a spike in contributions, I'm willing to press the Almighty for better terms."

With even Heaven primed for PORKYS, it remains to be seen whether the Chinese will buy off on the God-as-Underwriter concept given their longstanding atheistic stance, not to mention their surfeit of little green pieces of paper festooned with an 'In God We Trust' motto. Indeed Sinologists fully expect a debate within Party leadership circles, but only when forty consecutive days of rain can be verified.

One Wall Street financier who wallows in rapacious greed for a living confessed: "Of course if we're ever faced with the unthinkable—a foreclosure of Heaven—there's the Mephistophelean option. That would be a deal with the devil. But the amortization's a bitch and the thirty-year term feels like an eternity."

Betraying a fondness for *Paradise Lost* and those insufferable Miltonian quatrains, the Devil was quick with his own trite refrain:

> Work. The third-world does it better.
> America's the first-world. Why not let her
> get about the business of her fun?
> The credo? 'Let no daydream go undone'!

HE WHO CONTROLS THE SEARCH CONTROLS THE FUTURE

The future—as we've come to know it—may soon be a thing of the past. That's if the computer industry gets its way. By most accounts, Google is out front. 'We realized early on that fortuitous happenstance played havoc with our algorithms. The only way to sustain our nosebleed valuations was to control the course of human events.' So said Google spokesman Dash Balder at a recent industry trade show. According to Balder, Google plans to begin staging reality as early as 2006. The cost advantages are compelling. "Manufacturing information out of thin air IS the future. Wall Street is thrilled with our new strategic direction and cost structure."

Industry watcher Max Pariah concurs. "Google's developers are devouring the summation of all human history at the staggering rate of nearly a century every four months. Soon they will exhaust even the most arcane data. The search industry is months away from hitting its version of the sound barrier." Already, competitors are gearing up for what promises to be a bruising battle. "Google decided the only way to remain one step ahead of MSN Search was to create the steps in advance," Pariah explained, "the past cannot support a forward PE of 130 all by itself. Either you gotta start making things up or expand into stuff that hasn't happened yet. We feel seizing the future is the only way to press ahead."

Loathe to live in the past and having long since ceded the present to effete French existentialists, the future appears determined to recover lost ground. Google's Product Manager for Senseless Acts, Jack Ripper has noticed an up-tick in the future's activities: "We're already seeing a six-month backlog of serial killers. Frankly, there's a shortage of shallow, unmarked graves." Said one exasperated psychopath in an apparent desperate cry for advance notice "please index me so I can begin my grisly trail of carnage."

Colin Ferrell has already agreed to play the killer, "I think the movie will offer a riveting glimpse into the mind of a developing sociopath," he beamed. Google will allow Oliver Stone to begin pre-production simultaneous with the killer's deadly toll of human destruction. "Our madman is literally frothing at the bit. We're really excited about doing a movie based on a looming heinous crime spree," Stone said. Meanwhile the critics are poised to rave. Roger Ebert has signaled his intent to offer one thumb up. Unfortunately, the late Gene Siskel's replacement was unavailable for comment since no one could remember his name. Oddly enough, a Google search for 'the late Gene Siskel's replacement' came up dry.

By contrast, Microsoft has been much more low-key about its plans. Reached at his Redlands office, Bill Gates was cryptic at best, saying only, "I knew you were going to call. Would you care to review the transcript of our pending conversation?" As it turns out, Microsoft has copyrighted large swathes of the 21st century. In fact, 2035 has been set aside in its entirety as a General Protection Fault. At a recent trade show, Gates conceded, "It [the future] was a natural horizontal integration for us. Having thoroughly ransacked the past, stealing the future was our next logical step." Industry kingpin Larry Ellison was equally boastful: "We knew an arbitrary and capricious future would one day concede the inherent superiority of the relational database model. Why do you think we called ourselves Oracle?"

Seeking to avert the Betamax/VHS debacle of the 1980's, the industry has pledged, publicly at least, to support the interoperability of all competing visions of the future. But Microsoft's Sr. VP of Foreknowledge, R. Eddie Thayer, sees great promise in what he calls a 'split-screen' rendering of events: "We've always been a nation of second acts. In a two-search world, everyone will get a second chance. The industry is merely confirming a venerable American tradition."

Independent industry watchers are more sanguine however. Media prognosticator I. C. Roughly warned, "I think we could be moving towards a bifurcated future branded across search engines. Increasingly, imminent historic figures will license their pending achievements to one database or another. History will become just another cable channel." When reminded there already was a History cable channel, Roughly got all flustered and ran out the room.

In a sure sign of trouble ahead, the legal establishment is positively elated at the prospect of a shiny new tollbooth. The ABA's Director of Fresh New Deep Pockets, Bill Liab pointed out, "Technology is fueling a trend that should lead to cascading billable hours. As people opt for double lives, we will enrich ourselves commensurately." Liab sees a world where lawsuits will one day collect treble damages—twice. When pressed to elaborate, Liab threatened to sue.

But he may not be too far off the mark. Already one man is fighting bigamy charges on the grounds he exclusively licensed his second set of vows to Lycos. Separately, John Hinckley is petitioning the courts for unsupervised visits on the grounds he only shot President Reagan in Google. Reached for comment in his psychiatric cell, Hinckley explained, "In MSN Search, I'm a horticulturalist with a penchant for collecting butterflies. Where's the crime in that?"

Even the Justice department is taking notice. Recently it announced the formation of a Quantum Physics group to analyze the anti-trust implications of corporate prescience.

Indeed cultural ethicists predict no sphere of human endeavor will escape unscathed. Already, the ripples are being felt in traditional family circles. One distraught man, unable to find himself on Google, conceded that, in all likelihood, he's barely here. A minor celebrity in his own hometown, he opined, "I'm hopeful the upgraded Microsoft product will find me. Otherwise I don't know what to tell my wife. Maybe I should just read the writing on the wall, bow to the future and disappear."

THE STALLS OF POWER: DON'T TAP, DON'T TELL

In the latest installment of his queer bid to retain power, Senator Larry 'the Lizard' Craig has reached a compromise with his scrupulously heterosexual Senate colleagues. In a step certain to unleash torrents of diarrhea and incontinence at the highest levels of government, the Senate Sergeant at Arms will forthwith be accompanying Craig on all visits to the Senate restroom whenever the Senator expresses a need to 'shake hands with an old friend'.

This protocol bears a striking resemblance to the grade-school practice of raising ones hand during class in order to receive a ridiculously large wooden key-pass for the sole purpose of traversing the school halls, unmolested, to the restroom. Alas some practices are never fully outgrown, even for the powerful found peeing in our midst.

Constitutional scholars are far more withheld. Said one, "frankly, what a duly elected official chooses to do in the privy should remain privy to his God, his illicit gay lovers and his Political Action Committee." Ironically public restrooms accommodate some of the last remaining cubicles of free expression in America. Surprising many avid potty-watchers, the Republican majority (at the time) failed to capture public restrooms within the sweeping new surveillance powers of Patriot Act II, prompting many to ask whether this was a genuine oversight or the cynical erection of safe havens notorious for being short on toilet paper—and long on Republican loiterers. There's no question Republicans have traditionally applied a broad interpretive litmus to the public restroom. Asked this very question, former President Bill Clinton, himself no stranger to right-wing conspiracies, replied, "shit if I know" before bounding off to deposit some old beer of his own.

Affectionately known for encouraging a sort of awkward camaraderie, urinals do enjoy their share of jocular support. So perhaps special standing is warranted. But frankly, whether a guy chooses to make a looping figure-eight, take aim at the American Standard logo or recite baseball stats over his shoulder while pointing Percy at the porcelain, he is entitled to his free-form eccentricities. So hands off Justice Thomas and keep that Coke can where everyone can see it. If only Craig had shaken his Idahoan potato-stick in a proper line-up of god-fearing, bladder-relieving men.

Oddly enough, the Senate compromise threatened to stall in the wee hours when Craig insisted he 'had to go really really bad.' (The early ground rules had prohibited Craig from using the facilities prior to banging out a sweet deal, even if the ostensible reason for the visit was a really big wizz.) According to one loose-lipped source identifying himself only as Deep Throat 2, the *commodus operandi* will work on a 'need to go basis' in the following manner: all bathroom visits 'expressly to the Senate urinals will remain fully in the capable and familiar hands of Craig himself'. To expedite matters, Senator Craig will signal to the Sergeant for a 'number one' or 'number two' by holding up the requisite number of fingers at the back of the Senate gallery. Should Craig ever depart from a stated number one visit—midstream as it were—and elect instead to troll 'in, near or around' a Senate stall, not only will his wet shoes be a dead giveaway, but he will be jeered at vociferously by a bipartisan coalition of Senate colleagues who hanker, compulsively it seems, for fresh new ways to lower the tenor of the national debate despite gratuitous pissed-off protestations to the contrary.

For his part, Craig has agreed to wear Dr. Scholl's reinforced rubber insoles to mitigate any sounds that could falsely be construed, in the words of his attorney, as 'inadvertent lewd and lascivious tapping'. Asked to comment on the largely testosterone-dictated compromise, Senator Dianne Feinstein—former mayor of San Francisco and by some reliable accounts a woman—sighed "at their best, boys will be girls." Senator Barbara Mikulski expressed a far more longing envy in her observations: "I wouldn't touch this barge-pole with an undercover sting—though there have been many times I wish I had a barge-pole."

Indeed social commentators are reporting a great silent pall befalling America's men's restrooms in the wake of Senator Craig's fey missteps. Watching her husband shuffle reluctantly into a local mall restroom, clutching a *Soldier of Fortune* magazine, Mrs. Sally Loo noted ruefully, "Normally I hate it when he drags his feet. Today though, I understand. Some small crevice of trust, his very manhood, has been frontally assaulted. It'll be a long time before I castigate him again for prematurely wearing out perfectly good shoes."

Other Americans were quick to render their graffiti-laced verdict. In a refrain observed at Joe's Truck Stop (I-81, Exit 23b, stall #3), one constipated wag scrawled, just to the left of the ubiquitous Seymour Butts drawing:

> If the Sarge hears no tinkling
> that's surely an inkling
> the Senator's clearly amiss.
> (Meet me at 7
> October 11
> right here where you're sitting.
> Love, Chris)

Great bowels of fire and God bless (or is it help) America!!

IT TAKES ONE CHILD
TO RAZE A VILLAGE

Stealing a page from eenie-meanie-minie-mo enthusiasts, the nation's leaders are fast at work dividing the population into two sprawling camps: the Watchers and the Watched.

When one moron—armed only with inalienable rights and a book of matches—can set fire to half of California, the necessity for round-the-clock, one-on-one surveillance of every American, or in this case, every other American becomes clear to all parties. That may explain why this public policy shift hasn't exactly drawn a firestorm of protest.

Cultural questions abound though. Are self-starting briquettes a little too idiot-proof? Did Smokey the Bear over-interpolate the relative sanity of his mammalian cousins? Is ranging pyromania the inevitable dark twin of rugged individualism? History has shown that no government by itself can suppress a tidal wave of pathologic behavior. Restoring national security will require a still more claustrophobic paradigm than even the Nanny State can offer: that would be, one fire chief for every Indian.

To that end, the Census Bureau has been tasked with identifying the top 150 million 'control freaks exhibiting fascist tendencies' in America. Selection criteria include returning Blockbuster videos at least a day early and observing Walk/Don't Walk signals even at deserted intersections. Smokers are precluded from Watcher status altogether, as are the vast majority of Californians.

The actual pairings will be derived via a rigorously complex, social-engineering algorithm developed by off-shore Indian engineers and held under lock and key by one of those accounting firms used at the Oscars and complicitous in the Enron debacle. To forestall charges of favoritism and nepotism, one government official vows that "no one will be his brother's keeper". Amen to that.

Even President Bush is on board. "I don't like social engineering. Then again, I didn't like nation-building either. So bring it on!" For her part, Ms. Norma Kline, retired librarian from Duluth, Minnesota promises to monitor the President very closely.

Even some libertarians are conceding that the all-too terrifying prospects of the 21st century are proving the death knell of unfettered freedom. It's as if the venerable maxim 'live free or die' stared into the abyss and returned chattering like a frightened monkey 'live free *and* die'.

One distinguished libertarian described the reversal more artfully: "By creating a formidable grass-roots security apparatus, the proposed National Watch Program does a good job of addressing the asynchronous threats posed by religious whack-jobs, garden-variety imbeciles, community college aspirants, avowed nihilists, chain smokers and teenage mutant celebrities. If Lindsay Lohan can—theoretically—sober up long enough to devise an IED, it follows that everyone in America is both a potential threat—and a potential victim. The Jeffersonian notion of freedom has reached a post-modern cul de sac. Our very survival now depends on studying each others' every move."

But the modern police state, even when conducted at the grass-roots level, is no panacea. Bleary-eyed atop an undisclosed, highly-fortified, mountain compound with a ton of screens, Big Brother was recently overheard muttering about the "futility of omnipresence" and demanding a vacation. Even the fascists are discovering the center cannot hold.

The economic implications are no less daunting. For example, The Stagflation Club points out that, with every other American relegated to *de facto* social worker status, the real work of nations—

hard, sweaty stuff such as building trains, planes and automobiles—falls increasingly to a bunch of demonstrable momos. Even under a regime of unprecedented supervision, experts are bracing for a surge in suspicious shop-floor fires.

Remarked one resident Club scholar: "All tangible outputs of labor will have to be out-sourced to nations whose work forces are frankly too hungry to start fires. Here at home, our plates will be full watching one another with a mixture of wariness, dread, flame retardants and plummeting productivity. If we persist in meaningful, sustained labor, the whole damned place is liable to burn down. The choice is as stark as it is impenetrably smoky. This nation needs to decide what it wants: measurable output or the charred remnants of former communities."

Thus goeth Liberty. Earned in blood by the few, burned with Zippos by the many. As Ben Franklin sort of said, any society that values the Patriot Act over arson deserves Santa Ana winds.

THE GLOBAL CONSPIRACY AGAINST SHIT JUST HAPPENING

I'm not a grassy knoll kind of guy. Inertia is the real king-maker on this planet. That, and jaw-dropping incompetence. In an effort to tack meaning to the morass, some poor souls seize upon intelligent design. But the grim reality is that no one's in control, no one knows what the hell's going to happen next and no one is pulling the strings. This comes as horrible news to many as being a pawn in somebody's diabolical scheme promotes at least a sense of belonging.

The truth is, our universe is a little light in the loafers. There's a lot of matter unaccounted for. In non-quantum physics parlance, this means a lot of things just don't matter. Conspiracy theorists should be wary about lashing every little thing to the mast of a sinister plan. They should be wary, but they never are. Massively complex conspiracies attempt to bring sense to even more massively complex realities. Compulsive over-thinkers, conspiracy buffs cannot bear the thought of a vast unscripted universe. For them, paranoia is a welcome respite from unfocussed existential angst. The dirty little secret is that most conspiracy theorists would rather fight than quit their imaginary oppressors.

Others skip the middleman entirely and point the finger at God. After all, he is the Prime Mover. I agree He moved—but to a better neighborhood, one with greased pulleys and well-oiled transitions

(Though I still capitalize His pronouns just in case.) You see, fellow four-dimensionalings, word from the next-best parallel universe is that God dumped free will and decided to go all deterministic with beige curtains. Mind you, I wouldn't trade our crimson shades for anything. They go so well with the blood-stained carpets.

So forget about a Grand Design. Life isn't a movie and it sure ain't grand. Quite the opposite, movies are the ultimate conspiracies against real life. It's not even a horse race as *mise en scene* beats stupid-shit-just-happening every time. When was the last time anyone bought popcorn to watch the random unfolding of events? If truth be told, real life—that craggy montage of fits, starts and awkward gestures—envies the hell out of movies. Perhaps movies are what life could have been if it'd only hooked up with a better agent. Oh well, Spielberg 1, God 0.

You've seen the movie: Frantic movie star is running down the hall intent on averting the complete destruction of the world as Hollywood knows it. Trailing him in lab coats, clipboards at the ready, are an ethnically diverse array of experts-who-clearly-have-their-shit-together. The star is barking orders and peppering his entourage with questions. The experts, never missing a beat, fire back answers with impeccable, machine-gun delivery. The movie star fashions an ingenious plan. The world is saved.

For anyone who's ever worked in a real-life organization, it can take days just to set up an email account. So I dismiss this sort of uber-competency out-of-hand. Movies get away with being so cock-sure of themselves because no director in his right mind would begin filming without a foregone conclusion. In a movie's small universe, everyone already knows what's going to happen. So they act accordingly. This teleological certitude gives movies a huge advantage over real life where a new script is delivered with the morning newspaper.

This all comes as news to conspiracy buffs. Forever trying to stuff life's genie into a movie-bottle, they plot away completely oblivious to their huge debt to Hollywood. Every paper cut becomes further evidence of foul play. Meanwhile the very glue of the human condition—abject terror, complete surprise and epic stupidity—are given short-shrift. The paranoiac's cascading 'malice of forethought' allows for no accidents.

But are we to believe the same guys who couldn't build a seawall around New Orleans architected the 9/11 tragedy as some kind of fiendish inside job? That's right. The Internet and magazine-racks are abuzz with all sorts of CIA-laced 9/11 conspiracies. Somewhere in purgatory, the ghost of Lee Harvey Oswald welcomes fresh company.

Did you know the recently-revamped (and thus emptiest) wing of the Pentagon was intentionally hit so that the conspirators—many working inside the building—would not be killed? Here's another: the conspirators *intentionally* chose 9/11/2001 as the strike date in order to coincide with the anniversary of the Pentagon's 9/11/1941 groundbreaking ceremony. Man, what a bunch of sentimental lugs. Or was this an *intentionally* selected date thereby planting a coincidental seed for future conspiracy theorists to pore over? Then there's this: on 9/10, a conclave of small gray aliens was seen high-fiving one another in a popular K Street watering hole, clearly relishing the next day's horrible events. Okay, I made the last one up. Then again, maybe I didn't. On the fringes of this fringe movement, there is someone out there who has already tossed extra-terrestrials into the 9/11 mix. The point is that in the highly deterministic world of the conspiracy theorist, everything is governed by intentionality. Or, as Spielberg might say, every scene must count.

But you can't have it both ways. Government types are either world-class bumblers or they have every little thing in hand. Conspiracy nuts clearly fall into the latter camp. They think the guys in charge really are in charge. By falling victim to this spectacular naiveté time and again, they badly misconstrue the power of the powerful. But at least their heads hit the pillow every night feeling someone's in charge.

THE PUPPET MASTERS OF BALL

It's an open secret. You can't keep anything secret anymore. Forget those nefarious cabals that operate at the highest echelons of power and influence: The Trilateral Commission, Carlysle Group, Elders of Zion, Knights Templar, Illuminati, Masons, Rosicrucians, Hermetic Brotherhood of Light, Opus Dei, Food Network Platinum Membership Program. Common folk of more mammalian temperaments—Elk, Moose, Lions—ask simply, when will the trains run on time? Fair plebian question, that.

Mind you the societies listed above represent merely the tip of a megalomaniacal iceberg. These particular ones come to mind mainly because of their aggressive membership drives. Often the hook is those blasted magazine subscriptions (Don't worry if you got suckered into *Family Circle*. It gets sent to a secret location anyway). I mean, look at the bulging roster of secret societies. Who *doesn't* belong to one? I'm not complaining. Everyone should be a malevolent hooded figure at least once in his life as it breaks down inhibitions. But already paranoid readers are questioning the rationale behind the aforementioned secret society list. Where's the Mystical Order of the Temple of the Rosy Cross, they ask warily? And don't ask how I know you're asking. Let's just say I can't divulge everything at one rendezvous.

Lucky for you I'm in a pretty expansive mood. But you must first promise to keep this diatribe strictly 'for your eyes only' (and no doubt at some point Google's too—search terms: *secret*— *very very secret—extremely secret—super-duper secret*). The fact is, there's a really truly very secret society that wields unrivaled power over our dreary, insignificant lives which, frankly, don't amount to a hill of beans anyway, so why all the fuss to control them in the first place?

But I'm letting my own crushing anonymity drive us off-point. In fact this secret society is the envy of all other secret societies as the former, due to a spate of high-profile movies, couldn't get arrested in an undisclosed location anymore. Call it Delphic envy or da Vinci Code hangover. Are you leaned in close to your screen? The society is *Dull and Drones*. Shhh. If I had a proper black-ops budget, your computer would be turning into a gnarly stew of medium-well motherboard and toasted circuitry about now. But I don't. So be quiet. Or else.

Now that I've raised my kimono a bit, it's your turn. How about a credit card number? Hah. Just kidding. My associates can obtain that through any number of surreptitious sources. Anyway DnD is so secretive that most members don't know where to send their dues. Others have no idea a complementary coffee mug awaits them on an impregnable island-fortress in the Adriatic Sea. This rather vague affiliation makes plotting the course of human affairs problematic to say the least.

Secret societies also enjoy a certain cache, albeit an oddly unraveling one. For no sooner does someone get in than he brags about it to his buddies over too many beers and, *voila*, it's not a secret anymore. By this same drunken logic, you should never hire an aimless drifter to do a contract killing because invariably he will boast about his exploits in a seedy bar when the unsolved case pops up on America's Most Wanted. Emboldened by copious amounts of beer, horrible self-esteem lashed to sociopathy can yield a raft of unintended consequences. I mean, why not just volunteer for a life sentence why don't you?

DnD is far too clever for that sort of pedestrian crap. Their mandate is as cunning as it is two-pronged: 1) secure political power in the hands of a tight-knit band of glorious assholes and 2) dispense with stupid secret handshakes that never seem to work anyway. Most secret societies revere a wise man, usually some manic-depressive son of a bitch who swears his paranoid-schizophrenia is a diaphanous conveyor-belt to transcendent Truth with a capital *T*. A nut-job in short. DnD doesn't embrace a personage as much as it does an ethos. That ethos is Shameless Fucking Ambition, often leavened with Never Putting Your Own Ass on the Line.

Through alchemical sleight-of-hand drawn from the sublime well of arcane esoterica and held fast by a bent coat-hanger wedged in the doors of perception, the DnDers have managed to curve time and space to render truly startling and counter-intuitive outcomes. For example DnDers rarely take up arms, at least not in a manner that would tempt personal peril. But they are famous for marching others into battle and they can sing the National Anthem like the dickens. Sticklers on the finer points of valor might call this hypocrisy—a nuance that, historically, has been lost on the vast majority of frothed-up proles looking for the next good fight. When pressed on the point, the typical DnDer response is 'shut up and keep looking over there.'

Here's another one for the Hall of Mirrors Hall of Fame: DnDers can take a political adversary who actually served in battle and make him wish he'd dialed in AWOL. No one knows how they do this exactly. But there's an evil genius or two who wants the formula. In fact DnD's branded cowards would fill a small American Legion banquet hall: George McGovern (decorated Navy fighter pilot in Korea, later deemed a wimp by Nixon's cronies), John Kerry (one of Vietnam's swift boat casualties—years after the war's conclusion), Max Cleland (former Senator who lost three limbs in a grenade mishap in Vietnam only to be lambasted for his 'clumsiness' by talk circuit warrior Ann Coulter on the premise that technically he was not disabled via direct combat.) Bona fide wartime experience can get you into a real pickle these days particularly from those whose passion for a strong America is so all-consuming they never get around to taking up arms themselves.

Either there's pernicious mind control at work on the sinuous and subtle noggin of the average American or our minds have become so flaccid that glaring contradictions now fail to register in the collective semi-conscious. If the latter, then the string of education initiatives launched over the last twenty years have yielded spectacular results. In fact it may be the ease with which we're led by the nose that's become the worst-kept secret of all. But please don't tell anyone I shared this information—at least not while my membership with a certain hush-hush organization is under review.

QUAYLE HUNTING

Rumor mills were abuzz in the Nation's Capitol yesterday over the White House's 24-hour news black-out regarding the Cheney 'hunting accident'. Not since Richard Nixon's infamous 17 1/2 minute tape-gap has Washington engaged in such fevered speculation over a span of lost time in the executive branch of our government.

Adding to the mystery was the assertion by one unnamed SS agent that he heard a second shot emanating from a location to the left of the Cheney hunting party. Was Dick Cheney the lone gunman? Ballistic experts are skeptical. "The injured man's face was a patchwork quilt of lacerations. No single burst of buckshot could account for the extent of those injuries." So said former ATF expert Shel Casing. Adding to the confusion are eye witness accounts from three separate and unrelated individuals placing Dick Cheney in Dealey Plaza at the time of the alleged accident. Said Mavis Beacon, "I saw the Vice President leaving the Texas Book Depository with an armful of Criminology text books. I'm not sure what he would be brushing up for. But it was him, I'm positive."

At the time this story was filed, various Mafioso crime figures with a potential axe to grind had not been reached for comment as they were either dead, in jail or auditioning for Martin Scorcese's upcoming gangster pic. To some, the eerie silence from organized crime only deepens the mystery.

While sympathetic to the media microscope his fellow Republican is currently laboring under, former Vice President Dan Quayle was unusually introspective: "Look, as a former occupant of that office, I feel for Dick. But on a personal level, this tragic incident re-opens old wounds. Once again, my family and I find ourselves the targets of late-night comics. It's bad enough that the bird species shares our surname. But the fact both share a common spelling, well, that only adds salt to a wounded potatoe."

READ OUR LIPS

—Presswire, Sacramento, August 11

Responding to mounting pressure for intelligible gubernatorial candidates, the California General Assembly pushed through a bill this afternoon mandating elocution lessons for all gubernatorial aspirants.

"It's like a poll tax for the speech-impaired." Said Americans for a Garbled Message president Marshall Hum. "We're on the precipice of a slippery slope. I don't want to live in an America where I must be understood." Then, pausing for maximum rhetorical effect, Mr. Hum shouted "gabberwockyconundrumalice!"

Some of the more luminous candidates were even more poignantly cryptic in their damning appraisals. "The rain und Spain fahs mainly und da plain." Arnold Schwarzenegger recited proudly from a handwritten note.

"Vat dis need foh elocution dahhlinnk. I haff money!" exclaimed Arianna Huffington.

Even the White House felt compelled to chime in on the issue. When asked about the centrality of intelligibility to a vibrant, working democracy, President Bush muttered "My family has a long troubled history with lip-reading. As long as the fish can breathe, there is oxygen in America."

"This eleventh-hour drive for candidate intelligibility is a bullet aimed right at the heart of celebrity notoriety" huffed uber-Agent-turned-political-activist Rick Gold. "If the rich and famous aren't safe from the clutches of public discourse, mutes and stutterers can't be far behind. This is a dark day indeed for those Americans to whom we don't have the faintest inkling of what the hell they just said. Today I am not proud to be a Californian."

Political consultant Les Moore offered a similar assessment: "People know what (current governor) Davis is going to say before he says it. And look where it's gotten us. We need a candidate who means what he says, not necessarily one for whom we know what he means. Comprehensibility has been tried ad nauseum. It's a bankrupt political asset and an invitation to duplicity. Sacramento will rue this day. By passing this legislation, they are squelching the perfect political foil and a potent political paradigm for the future. An unintelligible candidate can promise anything to anybody and who will know?"

LAY DOWN, KENNY

I hope I don't embarrass Mrs. Lay unduly when I note that the Lay family is down to its last five homes. Sadly, the other eight have been sold in recent months to finance mounting legal bills and to pay off whoever is doing an exceptional job of helping us forget Kenny Lay. As Saddam Hussein once famously remarked, "when you're down to your last twelve residences, the walls have a way of closing in on you." How true.

Pity the Lay family as they grapple with such daunting new issues as paper or plastic (the domestic staff was put on notice weeks ago) and who gets the run of the 10,000 acre Wyoming ranch on Tuesdays. Life can get complicated real fast when the on-staff residential consultant suddenly packs his bags, leaving the family to juggle a bewildering array of sleeping options. Believe me, the rich have problems we can only dream of.

I had the rather bittersweet distinction of attending one of Mr. Lay's exceedingly well-publicized garage sales a couple of months ago. It was easy enough to find what with the big black magic-marker arrows scrawled on the back of Enron stock certificates. They were posted every few yards or so in a real tony section of Dallas.

As I was rummaging through a stack of old Osmond Brothers eight-tracks, I couldn't help but overhear Ken remark to his saint-of-a-wife Helen, "Dear, if our fortunes turn up again, do you suppose we could rebuild our cherished beer bottle collection? A Molson is a terrible thing to waste."

I didn't have the heart to tell him a Molson bottle in pristine condition could fetch $5.00 on e-Bay. Still, there it was with a $3.75 price tag on it. Hey, wasn't this the financial uber-genius who pioneered "buy low and sell high" via a bewildering array of algorithmically-derived, mind-numbing, hopelessly complex option derivative back-ender straddles? Had the California black-outs all been in vain, I wondered? Come on Ken, get a clue. $1.25 could buy you a nano-second of high-priced lawyering. You may need it pal, especially if Cheney decides not to run for President again.

Anyway, after some heated front-lawn negotiations, I ended up buying the Texas Rangers tea-set. But it was a $3.50 purchase made more from a sense of sympathy than from any real utilitarian need. My Elvis-in-Vegas setting does me and the kids just fine. Still, you gotta laugh at how old habits die hard. No sooner had we shaken hands on $3.50 than he offered to sell it to me for $2.75 in 60 days if I would let him use my cell-phone for one call right then and there.

Okay, I bit. Unfortunately, the Oval Office had changed its number with no forwarding recording. I hate it when people do that, particularly people in high public office. It's like they have something to hide. Anyway, I thought Ken was going to burst into tears. I gave him the $3.50, grabbed the tea set and me and my '92 Chevy Chevette were out of there, speeding back to the wrong side of the tracks.

Yes, I confess. I was feeling a sudden twinge of empathy for that suddenly hapless couple. After all, here is a guy who went from "Kenny-boy" to "Mr. Lay" in the flash of a public opinion poll. There was a time when selling your soul was like money in the bank, and enduring friendship—when fairly bought and paid for—lasted a lifetime. What's happened to this Walmart store we used to call America? It's enough to make this bargain-shopper cry.

THE BIG EASY HEADS EAST

When New Orleans blues rose up on cloven hooves to become a corporate profit center, it should have been clear to all watchful souls that the devil had indeed acquired Prada shades. Verily, all hope was lost. Every good little bourgeois knows it takes Midwestern Methodists like Hillary Clinton to raise a village-for-the-ages and sixty-minute waits for a table at the Decatur Street *House of Blues* does not even come close Bubba.

Not if Mother Nature has anything to do with it anyway...

That's why, reeling from the latest BP oil spill a mere five years after the catastrophic Katrina disaster, the State of Louisiana is considering geographical secession from the U.S. and a rapprochement with its old colonial benefactor, France, at a location approximately 300 nautical miles due-west of the Canary Islands. Constitutional scholars and geologists are divided on the feasibility of such a move.

This intrepid reporter found presently-charismatic-though-soon-to-be-paranoiac-island-strongman-in-waiting Governor Johnson in rare form. "The shrimp's gone. The gumbo's dead in the water. It's a bad neighborhood on the butt-end of a photo-op. Plus we're tired of American Presidents overflying our misery and playing sock-puppet to the devastation. Relocation to the eastern Atlantic puts us beyond the reach of Air Force One, tropical weather patterns and deep-sea drilling." Johnson continued, "That Sarah Palin can't find France on a map only provides an added benefit." Asked what the national food would be for the new island-state, the Governor huffed, "freedom fries...and South of France crawdaddies"

Before lapsing into all the usual French clichés, a spokesman for the Army Corps of Engineers expressed his department's position on the transoceanic move in unusually salty terms. "We busted our asses on that new network of levees, not realizing that *levee* was a French word. If secession happens, then I guess it's water under the bridge. But they're not getting our flotilla of camouflage-green barges. I say, send them up the gulfstream without a paddle."

To be sure, the logistical challenges are daunting. Al Qaeda munitions experts are expressing skepticism that sufficient IED's can be assembled and placed along the Arkansas, Texas and Mississippi borders to dislodge Louisiana from its neighboring states. However they're more than willing to help with the covert manufacture of said munitions. In the words of one operative, el Hussein "Pedro" Katani "we have a hundred crossing points along the Rio Grande."

As even the most geographically challenged high school student will attest, no state in the U.S. has ever physically extricated itself from the continental shelf of the Union; though reportedly Maine will be monitoring Louisiana's progress with keen interest.

Preaching characteristically against the choir, the Right Reverend Pat Robertson is not one whit surprised. "Next to Haiti, Louisiana is the worst place for voodoo and black magic. I swear to God you can't choke your chicken down there for fear it'll be fondled by some High Priest in a Santeria ceremony. Inflicting Job-like misery on Louisiana's already-poor and destitute is a sure sign of God's retributive hand. I saith, let Carla Bruni have 'em. We've got bigger catfish to fry."

THIRTY-YEAR PIN

Danny joined the group last month with about as well-scrubbed a face as one would expect from a 23-year-old with a $50,000 education loan. Man, you gotta love the exuberance of youth. He works diligently in a low-skill job, is unfailingly polite and has a relentlessly earnest quality that Corporate America likes to make short work of. His enthusiasm is all the more praiseworthy because Danny is a temp. Hey, one middle-aged man's cleaned-out work station is a younger man's sterling opportunity.

Just as the young can spot a half-full glass from a mile away, they can also drop some real gems. In this respect, Danny is no different from his peers. I don't know what $50,000 buys anymore, but it sure doesn't get you the word on the street. Career paths have been banned in the United States. It's right there in the NAFTA fine print beside the provision on Tijuana-manufactured baseball bats. No more paths or, for our South of the Border listeners, *el jobo vamooso gringo*. Pardon my Spanish. So it was with no small amount of shock that I found Danny approaching me after a couple of months on the job to inquire about his "career path" at our company.

"Career path", I asked?

"Yes," he replied. "Where can I expect to be in, say, five years?"

Suddenly, I didn't feel like the guy who signed Danny's purchase order funding in ten-day increments. How could I tell him that, only last week, we had had a spirited debate about whether to cut his position to fund a new coffee machine, the one that makes those piping hot cappuccinos? No, this was a young lad, awash in debt, asking me for fatherly advice about his future trajectory here at Fleeting Corporation, the third largest manufacturer of bowling pins on the eastern-Texas panhandle. I paused respectfully at the gravity of his question, gazing into my god-awful cup of instant coffee.

"Danny," I replied carefully, "it's a phenomenon that occupational behaviorists and plutocrats have been aware of for years: career paths promote a sort of idle complacency. People work more efficiently when they're scared out of their wits. Five-year planning is a privilege reserved for the filthy rich. There's a saying we use here at Fleeting: 'A long term scheme belongs to the man with green.'"

I continued. "The average American must live every day content in the fear that his or her job could fly out the window at any moment like a spooked Mexican fruit bat. As any sweatshop manager will tell you, fear is the juice that propels that last widget of output. Am I making any sense?"

Danny seemed flustered. But he persisted. "Mr. Jenkins, I've exceeded my pin quota consistently over the last couple of months. My pin-wobble-quotient is among the best in the division. Mine don't wobble AND they fall down."

I laughed. "Danny, I've seen your pins. They're good damn pins, son. You have the potential to make a great Pinhead here at Fleeting. It's just that, well, times have changed."

I decided to try another tack. "What do you think of our canteen, Danny?"

"Huh?" he asked.

"The lunch food here at Fleeting. It's partially subsidized, you know. Those cold cuts don't come cheap, I can tell you."

"Well, er, I usually bring lunch from home…"

I cut him off. "Danny, there's a factory just outside Mexico City that's beating our pants off. Their cost structure has us gasping for breath. Here, take a look." I guided him over to my office window that looked down on the plant below. "Tell me Danny, what do you see on the floor?"

He stammered, "Uh, lathes, packing machines?"

"Pin shavings," I replied, "Those infernal plastic shavings are everywhere, aren't they Danny?"

"Uh, yes sir, they are."

"Do you know that Mexican plant presses burger patties out of those shavings and feeds them to their workers at lunch?"

"What?" He gasped.

"That's right, Danny. The resin in the plastic apparently makes their workers hell on wheels. They literally have to push 'em out of the factory at night. They can't get enough." I laughed.

"How are you feeling Danny? Hungry?" I joked.

"Nah. More scared."

"Good boy. That's the Fleeting spirit." I laughed. "Now go out there and spin us some real knock-downers."

PROBING THE OUTER LIMITS OF INTERGALACTIC PROBITY (OR, "TAKE ME TO YOUR FEEDER FUND")

Fellow earthling, there is nothing wrong with your PC screen. Do not attempt to auto-adjust your A.R.M. and forget about those perennial paper tigers: Peak Oil, limited potable water and the prospects for yet another season of *American Idol*. There is only one notable alligator presently trolling the swamp of human fallibility: we have reached the terminus of low, easy monthly payments with no money down. Yes that's right. Having fully leveraged the intrinsic wealth of Planet Earth's three known—and garnishable—dimensions, the banking cartel is desperate for fresh skin in the game. That this skin may be iridescent and its occupant a cool 100 light-years away makes little difference in the present dire circumstance.

The crisis was brought into sharp relief at a recent conference of Quantum Cosmologists assembled, curiously enough, at the behest of the American Bankers Association. The dark matter on the table was this: How might sentient beings from alternate dimensions and parallel universes be cajoled into supporting debt levels they played no earthly role in amassing?

The leader of the conference, ABA's V.P. of Exogenous Markets Willie Loan, posed the inquiry thusly. "If there is sentience in any of these dimensions—and provided they are not the most attentive guardians of their otherworldly investments—we could recycle Fannie and Freddie paper *ad infinitum*. In short the shell-game is limited only by the audacity of our greed, the veracity of Star Trek and the exploitive potential of extraterrestrial civilizations. At long last deep space could pay off. At any rate, I'm determined not to let this promising start slip down a black hole."

A spokesman for the mortgage community appeared also to be on Cloud Nine from Outer Space. "We've packaged and resold mortgages three or four times over. Frankly the Chinese are starting to recognize the same old addresses. As the system desperately requires a fresh injection of Greater Fools, clueless aliens offer the best shot at a fresh round of malfeasance and bad faith. The fees would be quite literally astronomical. If their SEC's are anything like ours, it should be like stealing M&M's from E.T."

Real estate for reptilians is not as farfetched as it may seem. One alien abductee reports his Little Gray nuisance has offered to curtail all future examinations if the victim only relinquishes his red-week time-share in the Poconos. In short, there may be an untapped market.

Tiring of space probes that beam back goofy information on the origins of the universe, NASA wants a piece of Earth's action. With this in mind, the SETI program has been retooled to beam those ludicrous lead-in advertisements for no-point mortgages and low interest rates to every corner of the known universe. So far there's only been one inquiry from the Alpha Centauri galaxy. Scientists think it was a misdialed number. However the program is young and only got its toll-free number last week.

If $e=mc^2$ has any game, time may be on the bankers' side. After all what's a thirty-year mortgage horizon to a civilization that's mastered intergalactic travel at near-speed-of-light? Earth mortgages could serve as a very small—and speculative part—of any fully diversified galactic portfolio. At least, so say the financial experts who vouched for the safety of 401(k)'s. And thank God past results are not a predictor of future performance. Though one seasoned Wall Street insider mused: "if they have access to tomorrow's *Wall Street Journal*, we're cooked. Then again, if they have access to the last year of *Wall Street Journal*'s we're in deep doo-doo too."

There are other benefits as well. Highly advanced beings may assist our understanding of Collateralized Debt Obligations (CDO), an esoteric realm that continues to befuddle CPA's from Peoria. Said one: "It's funny. We were reaching the conclusion that *CDO's* were the product of a twisted alien intelligence."

At times, even the underworld can over-think. Reached in the front seat of a 2008 silver BMW M5, reputed repo-man and loan-shark Jimmie Gonovan took an oddly philosophic tact. "Perhaps alien cultures have struggled with dead beats at earlier stages of their advancement. How do you squeeze blood from a stone if, at the quantum level, stones don't exist, and you left your baseball bat at home?"

One concern among conscionable types is that Planet Earth could acquire a reputation as a tawdry way-station where lizard-brained, alien-complexioned sleazoids like former Countrywide CEO Anthony Mozilo bury entire distant civilizations under mountains of debt. Then there's sheer logistics to think about. For instance, how do you nail a warrant-in-debt to a door of perception or garnish wages from a viscous, ethereal humanoid who, in defiance of all strictures of notional value, has gravitated towards pocket-less spangled jumpsuits?

Even as you read this, not only is your mortgage amortizing along quite nicely in this time-space continuum, but some of the best minds on the planet are tackling these thorny issues—for a heavenly slice of TARP funds. The richly-compensated ethicist-consultant community is shrewdly divided. Paid Ethicists Who Exist for the Enrichment of Ethicists (PEWEEE) insists with characteristic circularity "who are we to impose our puny ethical notions on other civilizations? Moral hazard may not survive General Relativity. Besides we have no aliens in our clientele." When pressed further on this point, PEWEEE Spokesman M. E. Hack blanched before fumbling for a dog-eared cue-card "Bankers are wonderful human beings. I would not hesitate to leave my children with them."

Summoning his most serious mock-serious expression, Treasury Secretary Timmy Geithner struck a very, very serious note: "I don't want to minimize the logistics of human usury as it seeks to hollow out the full expanse of the known universe. We may stumble. Heck we may even piss off a superior civilization with the power to explode our heads from vast distances like overripe tomatoes. But if our bankers don't find fresh frontiers to ply their parasitic wares, the whole Ponzi scheme known affectionately as Western Civilization could come crashing down around us. The future of debt peonage hangs in the balance. All the ill-gotten gains a tiny percentage of the human population has amassed over the course of centuries could vanish overnight. Think about the opportunity cost of all that exploitation."

Stay tuned. Only time and space will tell whether the Masters of the Universe earn their really cool moniker. We now return you to your previously scheduled mortgage coupon book.

POLITICAL ANIMALS

BATTLE HYMN OF A REPUBLIC

For years the dominant trope in American political discourse has been the Red-Blue divide. Indeed its very ubiquity is the first clue to diversionary intent. Why? If the media is hammering something home it's time to check the mailbox for the foreclosure notice because nothing they tell you with numbing repetition bears repeating. If it did, you could use it against them. Why ever would they be so helpful?

Tenth-grade civics class does a bang-up job of enshrining the two-party system as an all but natural formation within the American body politic. Nice little indoctrination there, fellahs. But really, subtract an Era of Good Feeling and some third-party dalliances and that just about leaves donkeys and elephants. The party leadership's aims are informed by the people 'down below' who claim the party as their own. Grassroots loyalty is maintained by delivering on shared objectives. Organizational coherence ensues. This verticalized conveyor is entirely consistent with how one might expect a democratic nation to conduct its political business.

However in America, always more republican than democratic anyway (lower case, please), the power alignment is increasingly reasserting its horizontal bias. On top are the powerful, distributed across Republican and Democratic ranks in a manner that conforms mostly to careerist impulse or familial succession (Bayh (D) begets Bayh (D); Bush (R) begets Bush (R); Murkowski (R) begets

Murkowski (R), etc.)

Beneath the powerful are the powerless, many of whom take to heart, God bless them, the aspirations expressed in the red-blue platforms. Ideological integrity tends to be more of a grassroots preoccupation. While the powerful generally disparage change, celebrate stasis and welcome career advancement, they are more than willing to stage passionate conviction for the cameras. Furthermore, they enjoy applauding the appearance of change as it fosters the populist notion—and helps diffuse the populist energy—directed towards improving the lot of those outside the power edifice. In reality, red-blue is a garnishment balanced on the trough of mass consumption; or, as Marie Antoinette might say, 'let them eat parsley.'

To be sure, reactionary change—if that's not too oxymoronic—suits the conservative powers-that-be just fine. If a century of progressivity can be rolled back under the aegis of change, then change it is—and more of it. However nothing in this badminton game ever has the shuttlecock leaving the staid, square field of play. The essential substance is style:

Cosmetocracy

Intent on showing strength and steely poise,
she flashed gold earrings in the last debate.
His muted tie played faultless to the ploys
of influence and fifteen-grand a plate,
Appearance is a feast for casual eyes
While substance sits like lint on a lapel.
Good character is Dior in disguise
As tailored lines assure us all is well.
It's clothes that make the policies today.
Accessories don't lag that far behind.
The mannequin's the future and the way
Beyond the wonk whose mastery is blind
To all that fashion promises mankind.
Skin-deep's for keeps and not to be maligned.

Far more instructive is to view the red-blue divide as an oscillating bi-polar coalition. At varying times, one party holds the titular majority in Congress or the Presidency. However the *sturm und drang* that traditionally attends the transfer of power between the two parties vastly exceeds the portentousness of the shift. When will those goofy conventioneers get a clue? Iambic pentameter rides to the rescue yet again:

Oscillarianism[1]

There's method in a pendulating creed's
propensity for kicking out the jams.
We set all clockwork to the wanting seed's
election of the phase. Forbearance damns
the led. The trick's to trigger tiny coups
from dogged principle, a vote for chance
no matter stripe. Incumbency's a ruse
for power cementing absolute advance
with serpentine constrictions. Swap the bums
for new ones. Rest assured the same old dirt
compiles for Blue as Red. Then bang the drums
forever (heads that roll collect no bribes.)
They play at change, these so-called warring tribes.

[1] *Os-cil-la-ri-an-ism* [Latin oscillatus, past participle of oscillare to swing, from oscillum swing.] A grass-roots political movement (launched on this very page) wherein a Republic's citizenry shifts allegiances between parties at seemingly inopportune and counter-intuitive moments with the aim of de-stabilizing the ruling class. This political philosophy's forebears include Dadaism, Chaos Theory, Burgess' Inter-phases, the Maoist notion of perpetual revolution and Josef Stalin's practice of purging friend and foe alike to foster a climate of pervasive fear and paranoia. The spirit of Oscillarianism can be summed up thusly: 'Strength through Inexplicability' or 'Toss the New Bums In.'

After an especially seductive vertical light-show (i.e. the recent Obama coronation and its attendant rock star vibe), the horizon-tally-challenged find themselves reacquainting with the system's strict proviso against transformational change as their man begins his dizzying and inevitable descent back to earth. The propagated myth of change having vastly overshot the rigid specs of the sausage machine, we are now officially in the symbol-reentry phase.

As the ideological *non sequiturs* pile up, the most committed doctrinaires are slow to part with their tattered blue kimonos. Smart people are always slow to admit their stupidity. Nonetheless The Valley of Death must be traversed. Here are two whoppers that essentially strip away any remaining hiding places: Obama escalated the Afghanistan conflict and he re-affirmed indefinite detention. Each is an ideological abdication worthy of Bush the Third status. Given these monumental decisions that cling so shamelessly to the status quo, who but the most intellectually dishonest (or politically self-interested) can be struck by anything other than the ideological uniformity of the Obama administration *vis a vis* its recent predecessors? Beyond stylistic flourishes and distractive, personal curiosities—today ethnicity, tomorrow, gender—nothing of substance ever changes. In Obama, the powers-that-be enjoyed symbolic portent with none of the bitter aftertaste. Too bad they're only allowed one first African-American president. Not to worry. Right now, a Stepford Wife is being groomed as the next demographic gatecrasher. Before she's done, Sarah Palin may in fact give Mussolini a run for his money.

I reference fascism (really, republicanism *in extremis*) because it is in the air, just as the masses are boring in on the root scape of their miserable goat: illegal Mexicans. While the teeming masses still teem, they must be courted even as their growing functional obsolescence is becoming disquietingly obvious. The present age of evaporating consumer credit, productivity-driven labor surpluses and shuttered factories is hardly a clarion call for more people. But given that the masses are already here, they must be managed. Certainly their collective immensity makes them too populous for easy dispatch.

The point here is that the trend away from democracy and towards republicanism is an inexorable flight back to centralized power. Increasingly during this period, the two parties resemble bureaucratic artifacts of a prior era when ideas enjoyed at least a modicum of sway over undifferentiated power. This republican retro-trend signals that a high-water mark in the enfranchisement of the individual has been reached. That promontory is now being given up. And honestly, who can get excited about individuals anymore? We are awash in them to the global tune of nearly seven billion. Serfdom, a historical term for extraneous humanity (or if that's too callous, individuals whose economic cost exceeds their economic value), could well become the vogue again. Wealth redistribution might rebalance things. But assuming a reinvigorated middle class, what would they consume and produce to sustain their class on a resource-constrained planet? Perhaps a ruinous world war looms ahead as properly diabolical medicine to cull the herd. The ascendant Orwellian paradox may be 'less is more.'

Whereas democracy strives to take account of all the people, republicanism curses itself for allowing so many to get here in the first place (be it via the birth canal or the Rio Grande.) The ominous question thus becomes: in a post-credit (and thus post-consumer) age, if the working man's sweat affords diminishing returns and acres of warm bodies are no longer required as bagmen to rationalize Ponzi-mortgage-paper for sale to gullible Chinese, what possible use does the common man serve in the numbers he currently comprises? The grim fact is that the economy doesn't need quite so many of us as it once did. The grim follow-on fact is that, no longer needing us, and yet for the time stuck with us, the need to control us takes on redoubled urgency. Piling onto this Malthusian vibe are issues such as environmental stress and the finitude of natural resources. For example forty per cent of the world's copper has been used up. Peak oil theorists argue that we are at or near the apogee of crude oil production after which a precipitous drop-off is assured. People require a lot of the stuff. But that's exactly what we're running out of.

As for the milling hordes, presumably they will not stand idly by and accept their existential redundancy without a fight. Nor, one suspects, will they be distracted forevermore by red and blue shell games. Surely the powers-that-be have a culminating project in mind? Some of the Internet's wild-eyed types claim the New World Order has already settled upon a nice manageable republic of, say, one billion earthlings. Yikes, that's quite a human haircut. It would however ameliorate a lot of societal and environmental pressures. But we'll leave that paranoid inquiry for another day, preferably before the Illuminati turn out the lights on that democratic-by-dint-of-distributive-processing scourge, the Internet. For the moment, if people acquiesce to the stylized power-sharing rituals and their interminable run-ups (the election cycle) in America, there is no hope in hell for real change. Clearly, credulousness is wearing thin on all fronts and across all ideological persuasions. So where's the revolution daddy?

For now, the political credo on both sides of the aisle involves preempting the onset of populist fury with more sound: "Don't just stand there doing little or nothing. Shout about it." Sayre's law, so often used to expose the essential triviality of academic disputes, is no less apt for today's national political scene: "In any dispute the intensity of feeling is inversely proportional to the value of the stakes at issue." Power has very little at stake in today's red-blue America. In part, that's why the rhetoric has grown so bellicose and ostensibly 'divisive'.

To belabor one 'side' of the rhetorical circus as an example, Fox News is a profit-driven entertainment (read: mass diversionary) complex that derives its sustenance from delivering anti-Democratic diatribes and demonologies to a lucrative niche market. Red meat sells. At least candor is refreshing. Rush Limbaugh, big fat bombaster that he is, makes no bones about his essential identity as an entertainer. Jon Stewart and Bill Maher are comedians with a more leftist shtick. That some people mistake their bread and circuses for intellectual citadels is a testament to the skill level of the entertainers, if not the dunderheadedness of the people.

No doubt there is great entertainment value in drawing lurid contrasts between the red guys and the blue guys. But where in the fine print does Obama even come close to Che Guevara? He's not even FDR (who, it bears recalling, was radical enough in his time that a fascist coup was contemplated.) The consolidation of power in America—a multi-generational, self-correcting, self-perfecting process abetted mightily in the modern age by media control and abundantly displayed in the steady re-trickling-up of national wealth—has managed to narrow the amplitude of even the gyratory head-fake that travels under the bumper sticker, *real change*. With remarkable skill, the system elevates pigs over men, the latter being excluded from entering the gates of the sausage factory altogether. The field of play belongs squarely to swinish aspirants. Oink. Abandon hope (and get a life while you're at it), all ye who demand a sirloin steak of a sausage factory.

As Sayre's Law further predicts, the increase in red-blue conformity has precipitated an escalation in inter-party rancor. Every hair is split to reveal a difference where no real difference exists. Older politicians are forever bemoaning the disintegration of collegiality and comity. The intramural bitterness so often exhibited today between and among the powerful is a compensatory attempt to obscure, entirely for public consumption, the utter triumph of the powerful over the powerless. It's a closed shop. But that doesn't mean the insiders can't pretend to fight for the guys on the outside. Politicians channel their constituents' anger in lieu of delivering substantive change because the latter has been taken off the table by the powers who gratuitously array their handpicked little piggies in battle formation. Gesticulation and theatricality have usurped fundamental change.

Reality cannot be kept at bay forever. As each fresh new 'change' candidate devolves into a 'same as the old boss' caricature, public cynicism ratchets forward yet another notch. This is why the powers-that-be must be contemplating what comes next. Certainly there is a race on to devise the ultimate soma cocktail of ignorance, complacency and stultifying entertainment. Moreover this proletarian stupor must be perfected before the cynicism wells up into mass unrest.

The industrial revolution begot the hospitality industry. In both instances, the impulse was unabashedly democratic: lots of people addressing the proletarian needs of lots of other people.

The reassertion of republicanism, after a brief flirtation with liberal democratic principles, is an ominous assault on the very notion of *lots of people*. Once upon a time in a world not so long past, the powerful relished lots of people because mass markets, properly served, could redound into unimaginable wealth for a lucky few. Furthermore as Henry Ford intuited, when the wealth is shared, markets enlarge allowing yet more wealth to become possible. Marxist overproduction was averted by enlightened capitalism, but only for a time.

A great wave of plebian credit was extended and parceled out to greater fools around the world, all in an effort to keep the wealth rolling. During this brief flirtation with the masses, certain rights and standards of living were extended as *quid pro quo*'s for production and consumption advances. Democratic ideals seemed on the verge of eclipsing republican prerogatives. Steadily, those same power interests are taking their parties back with torrents of money. Power is reasserting its jealous tradition of concentrating at the top.

Somewhere in Davos, the plutocrats can be heard muttering around their plutocratic table: "There are too many damned people." The gathering-back-up of political power is but an interim step on the road to something far worse. One wonders, what nature of rough beast—opiate or meat cleaver—have they devised to cull the democratic herd?

More Powerful Than a Speeding Ballot

Debate and bumper-stickers all for naught,
our democratic ritual's in league
with Gotham City rot. All can be bought
for pennies on the vote. Let's call it off
—this hope (or more correctly, wingless prayer)
that honesty will sidle to the trough
and make the case for government most fair.

Am I alone in thinking it quite daft
how super-delegates can fly away

like Superman endorsing Howard Taft
—despite *vox populi*—into the fray
of kryptonite and smoke-filled room intrigue?

Clark Kent knew this: within the changing booth,
all levers pull for power. Damn the truth.

SEZ ME

"*...men* were merely him-mimicking *things*, in the same category as other tools and stones. Always and unalterably his *I* must blacken the whole vault from pole to pole"—Richard Hughes, *The Fox in the Attic*

He is the boy who, never having had to cry wolf, suddenly finds himself pursued by a ravenous pack of them. How did this happen and is he equipped with the necessary tools to ensure political survival? As sharp teeth have not been required until now, it's fair to ask whether we have a fighter or an adept pleaser on our hands. Only the former will do. And yet in the wake of this boy-king's hurried ascension, we find ourselves asking the most rudimentary—and pertinent—questions *post facto*. It shouldn't be this way. Mesmerism clouded our judgment.

But first, a word on the matter of race; woefully overplayed, almost like a strategic diversion, it has stunted our examination of more pressing details. For example, the anti-intellectuals have much to dine on with an Ivy League professor at the helm. LBJ would have seized upon yet another feckless Harvard boy—-a Stevenson effete—getting a free ride. The best that can be said about the present leadership conundrum is that America has made real social progress. The election of Obama had aspects of a referendum, indeed of a coronation, as America sought to prove both to the world and to itself that it had overcome the sad legacy of racism. Obama benefited in incidental part from this expurgation. His presidency was one for the record books before it even began. Almost as an afterthought, we turn ourselves to the man.

Eisenhower's trial by fire was WWII. Obama's will be the office itself. Were we derelict in asking so little of him in advance? Child prodigies do not as a rule fare well in adulthood as character forms best in a cauldron, not in the lap of applause. There's something about the pedestrian dreariness of experience that dulls the preternatural shine of the boy-wonder. Obama's precocity is, frankly, a curiosity and hardly a qualification for the job.

Imagine that, once upon a time, Obama attempted, as most boys do, an *Open Sesame*. To his astonishment, the mountain face opened. Excitedly, he approached a larger mountain. Same result. After a series of triumphs over famously imperious terrain—Mt. Oprah, Mt. Kennedy—he became inured to his remarkable powers, perhaps thinking them his birthright. With the world perpetually falling at his feet, who could blame him? The feedback loop of self-seduction was established. While good fortune can confer impressive winning streaks, divinity should not be construed from an undefeated record. Even after a protracted period of levitation, reentry is assured.

There's also the complicitous madness of we the people. Life is never so unfair as to forgo a Door Number Two. Perhaps it's not announced with great fanfare. At the apogee of mass seduction, Fate deploys the occasional Isaiah to offer the voice of sober counsel. Ron Paul might be the present-day permutation of such a figure. Unlike the charismatic, however, a prophet's *bona fides* are measured by how poorly his words are received; think broccoli versus ice cream. Euphoria is a giveaway to false prophecy. Indeed the reality is as simple as it is habitually overlooked: If you are aroused by what you hear, then you are being seduced. Charismatics are canny narcissists. As our pleasure enables their power, they take great pains to tell us exactly what we want to hear. Illness answers illness in a dysfunctional symbiosis—if the latter is not too oxymoronic a notion.

Human nature is such that a true prophet's moral authority typically arrives in death when he can be lionized, safely enough, in a holy book. Despised in life, he is eulogized admiringly. The opposite is true of the charismatic. Nonetheless the faint voices in the wilderness are unmistakable: Beware the man for whom the world offers ready compliance. For he knows neither the world nor himself. He is a colossal mystery—both within and without.

Nature abhors the vacuum posed by hubris. Invariably, coaxed by some inscrutable contrarian cue, the world shrugs with inopportune delight. I fancy its disaffections manifesting in the *force majeure* of an avalanche. Some underling approaches him: "Sir, a faint rumble can be heard at the top the mountain." In the midst of receiving a batch of fawning dignitaries, the boy-king mutters distractedly: *Open Sesame*. Undeterred, the rocks continue their mad descent down the mountain-side. In his most commanding mellifluence, he utters the magic words again. By now, the sound of the oncoming avalanche is deafening. What god can hear the words above the din?

There is a look in his eyes these days, a dawning awareness of his receding powers. The curtain has been drawn back. But where is the warrior? Eerily, he seems to stand there beside us, inventorying the contents of the vestibule. A growing chorus of naysayers claims the vestibule houses little more than a microphone and a tape machine lashed to an infernal, platitudinous loop. A stubborn few suggest there is a darkened recess that has yet to reveal its contents. Others say he is a dirigible floated by the bankers, for the bankers. It is a matter of public record that they have been his paymasters to date. His Wall-Street-First-Main-Street-Maybe-Later prioritization is no accident to those with an abiding faith in the hegemony of the banking class.

Without question it will take more than mere incantations to alter the terrible physics set in motion. The forces are elemental; the response, to date, rhetorical. Are the words mere ornaments or does motive force lurk behind the incantations? More troubling is that charisma is a perennial precursor to tragedy *because the gods always withdraw their favors*. Sophocles' Silenus characterizes humanity's lot as being both wretched and ephemeral. There is something in the Dionysian dynamic of charisma that has all bacchanalias ending in a climactic frenzy of torn limbs. We can be transported from the wretchedness of unvarnished existence but only for brief moments.

Moreover the depth of our looming predicament is inversely proportional to the heights reached by our collapsing pleasures. The piper must always be paid. But my how he made us feel good while he enjoyed the god's favors.

The other alternative is that America has put the ineluctable calculus of Greek tragedy on permanent hiatus, you know, just as we overruled the Judeo-Christian prohibition against ruinous usury, the pernicious career of sin that gnaws at the roots of our society and which, to my mind, is responsible for the fast-approaching economic cessation. Deconstructing the metaphor, I'd hazard that the avalanche is the massive deleveraging of a decades-old Ponzi lending scheme that comprises the Western banking model. Greed, it turns out, was never good. Indeed for centuries it survived without challenge as a deadly sin. And what does it say about the end of the play when our current President is surrounded by some of Wall Street's finest real-life Gekkos? With gravity-defying hubris, Obama's patrons desperately want to revive the Ponzi (or what in more polite circles is referred to as the fractional reserve system, a sorcerer's apprentice ploy of creating multiplicative streams of money from thin air.) Certainly it would be a first. Ponzis never resume; they only collapse.

We are about to find out whether the boy-king's gifts are manifold or unidimensional. We should be very interested indeed as we are the sleeping village at the foot of the mountain.

WHEN YOU WISH UPON A CZAR

America's ruling class wants it both ways. Those in its ranks guard their power jealously. Eager to retain the perks, they nonetheless proffer a cavalcade of czars in hopes of shirking heavy lifting. Drug Czar, Education Czar, now an Intelligence Czar. The ruling class needn't bear the responsibility of ruling—give it to the czars. This autocratic fantasy betrays a subliminal recognition of the intractable morass American democracy has become. As it turns out, all the ruling class wants to do is dance at Inaugural Balls.

We tend to ascribe self-certitude to those in power, when in truth our Maximum Leaders are controlled mostly by their towering insecurities. Secretly, they yearn for the Übermensch, a Bigger Daddy who tells them what to do, administering sound spankings followed by prolonged house arrest with no VIP privileges. At least the trains would run on time.

Rarely, however, is the self-doubt of the ruling class so vividly evidenced as in "The 9/11 Commission Report." An eerily impuissant tone echoes throughout the massive tome, something like: "We, your leaders, are largely powerless to protect you." The report warns plaintively that 85% of the nation's infrastructure lies in private-sector hands. Read: "Our hands are full with the Statue of Liberty. Guard your own stuff." Yes, we're over the Rubicon without a Caesar. Next stop? Amtrak Czar.

Rumsfeld had it tragically reversed. The shock and awe is mostly ours. The world's only remaining superpower is discovering itself horribly vulnerable to flight-bound nail clippers. Though the report largely skirts the elephant in the living room (Iraq), there are the obligatory Beltway bromides about improving the "unity of effort" across disparate organizations, etc. But once again, the self-exploratory waltz of the well-connected (so euphemistically embodied—and entombed—in the "commission" format) converges on the same hackneyed prescription: "We'll appoint a cabinet-level strongman, 'cause he'll make us take our medicine."

The grass roots are equally parched. Americans are thoroughly fed up with their cache of personal liberties. In increasing numbers, they'd happily swap freedom for enhanced security. Funny how anthrax spores and suitcase nukes can shift the tenor of a debate. Breathing is, after all, the inalienable right, so who can blame people for thumbing their noses at the genteel postulations of a bygone Age of Enlightenment? According to Ben Franklin, those who relinquish liberty for a modicum of security deserve neither. But then, Franklin flew kites during thunderstorms.

Many Americans today would embrace Mussolini if it meant a copious supply of the first-run movies they've come to enjoy. What, too cynical? There is a move afoot in some circles to make Blockbuster Video the fourth branch of government. Strict constructionists, though strictly opposed, are treading lightly. Hassling America's largest dispenser of opiates would precipitate an uprising of massively obese proportions. It's thanks to Blockbuster that Americans have made permanent peace with the reclined, prone position. In this sense, Blockbuster is to Big Brother what John the Baptist was to Jesus: the Great Preparer. But what form will our new Messiah take, and will he generate sufficient box-office receipts? I don't know, but effete intellectuals would do well to sit down, grab some popcorn, and accept the inevitable. And no talking during the movie.

Grassy knoll paranoiacs get it wrong most of the time. I envy Michael Moore's childlike belief that someone in power has the world's problems completely in hand. If ending terrorism were as simple as disbanding Skull and Bones and the House of Saud, I'd relinquish my Yale decoder ring in a New Haven minute.

I miss the days when the seeming inoperability of our system didn't have such dire implications. The quaint term we used was "gridlock." Hearing it, our teeth would clench, each of us conjuring images of our own private purgatories. Rush hour was my personal demon. These days, sitting in interminable traffic, stewing over a continued lack of dictatorial prerogative, I reflect on the United States' utter lack of exceptional people in positions of authority. But then, that is what a generation of telegenic leadership can do. Mind you, good looks are not an entirely bad thing. As first lady in waiting Teresa Heinz Kerry bubbled recently, John Edwards is a babe magnet.

So who's our daddy? I can only tell you whom I would fearlessly follow up a hill in a battle for America's lost love of freedom. Trouble is that fearless leader mounted his (or her) last charge leading a group of fellow passengers to wrestle a plane into a Pennsylvania field. So who was that masked man? The greatest irony of all is that United Flight 93 had the belly of our beast in its sights. There, beneath a luminous white dome of indecision, that beast dithers even now.

NOW WE SEE YOU, NOW WE VOTE

"Want to be wherever nowhere will be, i.e. invisible!"—Kirpal Gordon, Eros in Sanskrit

Between Barack Obama and Hillary Clinton, I find myself tempted by the former for reasons that don't lend themselves to a cool reading of the facts. Am I caught up in a swell? In one of those odd moments of Jungian synchronicity, I stumbled over the following Baudrillard quote the other day: "Metamorphosis abolishes metaphor, which is the mode of language, the possibility of communicating meaning." Here was a clue. At the moment of change we are least beholden to meaning, to the past, to our accumulated disappointments. We are momentarily invisible to ourselves. This can makes us feel out of the woods. Out of body, out of danger. The contemplation of change can be an irresistible opiate.

This is not an uncompromising assault on change, but rather an acknowledgement of its enormously seductive qualities and attendant capacity for leading us astray. Of course change can be a pragmatic necessity too, as when we must stop smoking or risk the loss of a lung. But all too often the call for change is an abdication, a desire to escape dreary sameness. Who over the age of thirty-nine doesn't relish a clean slate? In this seductively charged context, the new circumstances can, in an odd way, be secondary to the enjoyment we derive when we move to embrace them—the great giddy rush of air that results when a tired promontory is vacated.

All too often, change is a sly riff on more-of-the-same, Eliot's 'gesture without motion'. We are plunged into a new regime, a fresh configuration of grinding realities. The danger is that, in the euphoria of acting upon our feelings of hope, the new conditions that we attain (hope's ostensible end) are not adequately considered. In fact the objective was never the changed condition per se, but the thrill of pondering a new identity in a new town. We crave hope and suffer change.

America has a yen for 'the change thing'. We entertain change so much because few things entertain us quite so much as change. The question that needs asking is, are we indulging change-for-its-own-sake or are we making well-considered strides towards a more promising regime? Bringing this philosophical preamble down to the earthly realm of presidential politics, is Obama—and to a lesser extent Huckabee—the logical beneficiary of a cathartic change in the body politic or are they the latest straw-men in America's all-out pursuit of the pleasure principle? Or, to quote Sam Vaknin's landmark work on narcissism, is Obama only the latest dirigible, America's current 'grandiosity bubble' almost certain to meet a Hindenburghian fate when the daily reality of holding office, with its myriad compromises, takes hold?

This will offend the transcendence-seekers, but a President's fate is tethered to the profane space that houses, for example, the business cycle. Quite unfairly, he either basks in the glow of prosperity or endures the epithets resulting from hard times. On the heels of the equity bubble bust, real estate values launched their own outsized ascent. An economic determinist might argue that Obama owes his current mantle of expectancy to the recent collapse of the sub-prime mortgage market. With the credit markets in disarray, perhaps he is the newest inflation, financial-engineering-made-flesh. Far from a seminal figure, Obama may simply be the latest symptom of a venerable disease, the latest evidence of America's reluctance to face a bubble-less horizon. Prozac, please.

The season turned like the page of a glossy fashion magazine.

> In the park the daffodils came up
> and in the parking lot, the new car models were on parade.
> Sometimes I think that nothing really changes—
>
> The young girls show the latest crop of tummies,
> and the new president proves that he's a dummy.
>
> —from *'The Change'*, Tony Hoagland

The other day on C-SPAN I watched Hillary Clinton getting roundly booed by Obama supporters. The most noise came during those moments when she offered her own rendition for bringing change to America. And this was at a New Hampshire State Democratic event. Hardly a hostile crowd, it was nonetheless an audience savoring the demise of an 'in-house' dynasty and relishing the prospect of change. But just how unpalatable had the Democratic status quo suddenly become? After all Hillary Clinton had been the crowd's favorite just hours before. What really had changed?

Later that evening, Republican pollster Frank Luntz assembled a room of New Hampshire voters to solicit their impressions of the Democratic debate held earlier that day (and after the event described above). Remarkably almost the entire room had switched from Clinton to Obama over the intervening days and hours. So much for Clinton's thirty-five years of public service on Democratic-friendly causes. That had all slid behind a storm in a teacup. The crisis du jour? Clinton's visible irritation with both Obama and Edwards' characterization of her as a status quo figure during the evening's debate. Inquiring minds wanted to know, had her arched eyebrow flashed anger, irritation, arrogance or entitlement? How could such an eyebrow be allowed to inhabit the Oval Office?

The seasoned New Hampshirites Luntz had praised only moments before for their unflappable Yankee rectitude had bitten the easy fruit of the last visual image. Obama had just turned in a better performance than Clinton. The flat screen of television had flattened the experience disparity with frightening alacrity. I should also note that Luntz has been accused of staging infomercials with actors posing as voters. The surreality deepens.

My next-immediate thought was that the butt-end of the present dynasty, George W. Bush, has, by way of an historically abysmal presidency unleashed a thirst for new beginnings beyond any sense of proportion—or partisanship. Suddenly the public's desire for change is like a flesh-eating virus. The status quo—any status quo—is prima facie radioactive. Bush has succeeded in putting even his committed enemies on the run to the extent that they, like him, labor under the burden of experience. Oddly, it's lame-duck Bush who has become the Clintons' worst nightmare with Obama the beneficiary of the anti-experience backlash. For avowed Clinton fans, it must be like having the baby thrown out with the bathwater. The fact that Clintonian experience may be required to counter the Republican mud-slinging machine in the general election is, in the current heated moment, an unexamined probability. After all there are many reasons to dislike the Clintons. But should George Bush be one of them? Could the change train be overreaching?

Certainly the current mood for change is as clear as it is veeringly reflexive. In a recent Charlie Rose appearance, Bill Clinton encapsulated the inherent unfairness of the prevailing calculus, arguing that, whereas Hillary was a proven agent of change, Obama was a symbol of change who had yet to demonstrate his effectiveness as an agent. Politically astute as ever, Bill was attempting to assuage what had become an unmistakable drumbeat: out with the old, in with the new, whatever the new may be.

The public's recourse to an antiseptic clean owes much to a Puritanic strain in the American psyche that whips up periodically with all the fervor—and mass hysteria—of a witch-hunt. Paraphrased, it is that worldly knowledge is the root of all evil. Resumes are the grates of accumulated ills and vices. Today's political pendulum is on a mission, perhaps even a mission from God—certainly if Huckabee prevails. Unfortunately we may be holding our noses right into a trap. Do I hear Keats' negative capabilities banging about? Huckabee and Obama are Jimmy Carter in stereo, the latter a politician elected on the 'strength' of being someone we knew practically nothing about. With this aversion to flesh, surely Ralph Ellison's invisible man will one day occupy the White House. Flesh out fantasy and it quickly betrays a nervous tic; the manifold disappointments of a pock-marked, peopled landscape. In his poem *'Dear Derrida'* David Kirby further plumbs the deconstructivist angle, suggesting that we may prefer that there be 'no them' as we've already concluded there is 'no us'. Weary of our leaders' asymmetric warfare, we yearn for a fresh symmetry, a face to match the untried potential of our own:

> …each was telling us that there is no us:
> that cultural structures
> or the media or Western thought
> or the unconscious mind
> or economic systems make us
> what we are or what we seem to be, since,
> in fact, we are not, which isn't such bad news,
> if you think about it, because it means
> we don't have to take ourselves so seriously…

Later on in the poem, one of the characters rejects the narrative's advice, opting with dead seriousness for the ultimate invisibility gig—suicide.

Where the uninitiated sees in a new face a pig-in-a-poke, a believer sees salvific potential. The Huckabee and Obama fevers have all the earmarks of flights of fancy or tent revivals. Underlining the intensity of the change theme is the fact that both parties are reaching for the back of the rack in the same election year. Who could have guessed the far-reaching power of a credit crunch and an intractable war? Had the incumbent Gerald Ford not run in 1976, what Republican change agent might have taken his place? And wasn't Ford, author of Watergate's final chapter with his pardon of Nixon, himself a human sacrifice to change? It's a testament to the vagaries of a mirage that Carter's and Ford's estimations as Presidents have fallen and risen respectively with the passage of time.

Political saviors are a reckless indulgence. It's a world-weary refrain, but shouldn't national crises elicit cries for experience? Connectedness, despite its pejorative connotation of backroom bargaining, will be crucial. Hit the ground running or die. You want a learning curve, go be President of Malawi. Things move more slowly there. You want a theocracy? Go live in the Vatican. We are also a consumer-driven culture more than we care to admit. This may further explain the outsized appeal of the outsider. However throwing naiveté at intractable problems often deepens the intractability (the Carter years). Obama could be a prodigy. For now all that can be said is that he and Huckabee are the newest of the new. Their shelf-dates notwithstanding, they will still be beholden to their respective parties where agents of change are routinely folded into programmatic realities.

We are in the boomerang phase of American idealism when we seek to inoculate ourselves from the world by finding the cleanest hands. During this phase, the notion that politics and dirt are essential bedfellows is ignored. America will not find the political savior it seeks in either of the major parties as the latter are well-oiled corruption machines. But please, no moralizing. It is what it is. And frankly, doesn't the world deserve an apology from Americans before Americans deserve a savior? Nor is morality bifurcated, especially in a society that, for all its ills, can still toss up 'unvetted' figures like Obama and Huckabee. The leaders and the led operate from the same moral compass. If 'they're all crooks', then so are we. The fact is they are what we would be if only we had their political connections. So enough sanctimony from the amen chorus. In a nation that spends approximately $10 billion a year on pornography, it's safe to say Puritanism is a bygone affectation. What guise would a political savior take anyway? Huey Long? Joan of Arc? Bart Simpson?

The business of politics does not yield readily to amateurs. Nor is denial-fueled idealism a viable path. We only end up idealizing the muck. The pragmatist asks, which venal politician aligns best with my own venalities—which politician will steer the country closer to my own or my children's plebian ends? These are the low-falutin questions that need to be asked. Currently they are being skirted. After Guantanamo and Abu Ghraib, Americans can be excused for wanting to sprint to a higher altitude. As forgivable as this impulse is though, it's still an impulse unleavened by rumination—or contrition. The crimes committed in our names will not be absolved by pretending we have a new fresh sheet of paper before us.

The world deserves the most qualified Americans we can find—now more than ever. Whether that qualification involves old-school experience or a clean break with the past is a question best left to the collective wisdom of the electorate. I have elaborated my misgivings without suggesting a superior candidate. However it would be yet another exercise in national self-indulgence to flirt with a seductive new face which, like all new faces, will earn its derision soon enough—for the newness of that face alone. What we need is a little less mad science from the Great American Experiment after a disastrous start to the 21st century. So don't get your halos in a twist folks. In the final analysis, they all suffer profound shortcomings as career party politicians. Cast off your wings, your fleeting desires, and with the steadiest of hands, vote your considered best for the future.

THE PRIVILEGED FEW
AND THE BUDGETED MANY

There's an apocryphal tale of John F. Kennedy on the 1960 Presidential campaign trail. Concluding an animated chat with a well-wisher, JFK turns to an aide: Why would someone endure a thirty-year ordeal of paperwork when it would be so much easier to just buy the house outright, he asks, you know, write one big check and be done with it? At which point, the aide explains to his well-heeled boss the usurious indignity known to most of us as a *mortgage*. Yes, the rich are different. But those who have wealth thrust upon them by sheer happenstance are surely the most different of all.

Our present-day Democratic pretender, JFK II, did not achieve uber-wealth by fortuitous bloodline, but he didn't exactly earn it either. John Kerry married it. Twice. At least he had to sell himself. George II is a virgin in the hustle and bustle of life's transactions. So what'll it be America, a silver-spooner or a gold-digger, because we're sure not getting a self-made man. There are many paths up the mountain. But the ascent is a lot easier when you can transport your loot in a ski-lift. Unfortunately, a dearth of rich widows makes PMI payments the norm for most of us. Still there's a consolation: we're building character even as we prop up the insurance industry.

George II, another stranger to the sweat of his own brow, likes to peddle the fanciful notion that he is a fiscal conservative. In truth, Bush is congenitally abudgetal to which Mayflower inbreeding may be largely to blame. You see, Bush began life with a budget-busting impairment. Everything was laid at his feet before he could utter a proletarian gurgle. When incipient needs are thoroughly anticipated by an overweening governess, personal bearings can suffer. The occasional hunger pang is like a beacon, teaching us real life skills such as where the refrigerator is and how to make a ham sandwich. Bush experienced no such pangs because he had a butler with a silver stethoscope who listened for the faintest rumblings in Boy George's tummy, and then dashed to the pantry for a cheeseburger. Everyone should be poor once in his or her life though I don't recommend making a habit of it.

The Bush clan finds itself miles above the "need thing". In some ways, this makes them lucky. In some ways, this makes us unlucky. Food, shelter, clothing and tuition, are you kidding? Not when your trust fund has a trust fund, Bub. While many of us were bringing macaroni and cheese to a slow boil, the Bushes were brewing a political dynasty with the Carlyle Group as dessert. Hey, it was either that or endless rounds of golf. George II's fiscal thermostat is not broken. It's just been bred out of him. This is the tale of how one man's good fortune can become a nation's catastrophe.

As *Meet the Press* Tim Russert noted recently, no less conservative bastions as the Cato Institute and The Heritage Foundation have deemed Bush "the biggest spender in American history." For those Republicans whose identity is lashed to the quaint notion of fiscal conservatism, Bush is an LBJ in sheep's clothing, an ideological non-sequitur. What, they were expecting mettle from this man? Where was it forged? The Skull and Bones treehouse?

Of course there is the tired supply-side pabulum: It's the people's money and cutting taxes in the face of growing deficits is economically stimulative. But George II lacks the Gipper's earnest conviction. Even the staunchest trickle-downers must be tapping their barometers 'cause we're in the Gobi Desert of fiscal unchartedness, folks. If Bush's 2004 campaign theme was hooked to a polygraph machine, it would be sputtering Orwellianisms: war is peace, love is hate, restraint is profligacy, deficits are prosperity. In truth, Bush can't feel our pain, try though he might. And why should he even try?

Red jerseys and blue jerseys notwithstanding, anyone with a passing interest in national solvency should take a renewed look at the old tax-and-spend Democrats. We need their budgetary discipline. At least Kerry's acquired family makes a fine ketchup, a Reagan-era dietary staple. Our grandkids' school lunch programs may need vats of the stuff before we see the back of this $7 trillion rich man's burden.

Let's review George II's current Santa's list...

We need a massive new agency to protect us from terrorism, fewer global despots, prescription drugs, a two-front military capability, a man on Mars, Star Wars, a Middle East Marshall Plan, lower taxes, even better manners. And we're gonna get them all. As Bush told Russert, "...I think it's important for people who watch the expenditures side of the equation to understand we're at war, Tim, and any time you commit your troops into harm's way, they must have the best equipment, the best training, and the best possible pay." Okay, it's tough arguing for an escalation in troop endangerment. George II deftly sidesteps the expenditure issue by draping it in a war-torn flag. Budget-wise, I'd say he's skating just like a rich kid.

But then, rich kids have the option to skate. The rest of us must chart a life course around and between the twin-pylons of desire and realistic expectation. If a person's character is largely defined by how he officiates his needs and desires, surely trust funds can blunt this self-regulating mechanism. As Aristotle remarked, character is plot. We either work for a new car, saving month by month, or we steal it. To hijack a Clinton-Blairism, there is a third way: it can simply materialize in the driveway on our sixteenth birthday.

No lineage starts out on top. Once, someone had to tow the line and establish the lucky sperm beachhead. Every family dynasty had a real smart, tough bastard who knew the value of a buck. We've all heard the stories of J. Paul Getty's mansion pay phones and John Rockefeller's lousy restaurant tips. In fact, show me a philanthropic foundation and I'll show you a guilt-ridden benefactor with a twilight spiritual crisis. Maybe Carnegie, after bailing out his rotten kids once too often, realized a foundation was the only way to avoid wholesale familial dissipation. Thanks to Carnegie and Mao Tse Tung, every town in America can now proudly boast a public library and a Chinese restaurant.

Then there are the working poor, the salt of our earth. Their work ethic is both momentous and sublime. Watching young kids toil at an inner city McDonalds provokes an odd reverence. Even the silly uniforms are like hare shirts, designed to invite uncool comparisons with their resplendent gansta peers. But character can be a pit bull, refusing to let go. Easy money, glamour, the thug ethos must be a tempting lifestyle when the alternative is $4.25 an hour. And yet, these kids get up every day to flip burgers. Talk about presidential timber not to mention character forged in the grease palaces of purgatory. For me, they are proof-positive of the mysterious fortitude of character, how it can sustain itself, day-in, day-out even on a steady diet of burgers, fries and stray bullets.

It's not that I have an unabashed admiration for the poor. Many of them are simply thwarted megalomaniacs on a shoestring budget. But the ratio of resources to needs can be so cruelly inverted as to practically guarantee despair. God help the poor and their peculiar set of dangers. America sets its highest bar for them.

Perhaps the largest repository of budgetary grit lies within America's besieged middle class. They wrote the ledger so to speak, sweating over it with every monthly bill cycle. Ask your average American family what a budget is. Chances are they'll offer up a poignant refrain such as passing on the kid's braces for a college tuition fund. A family budget is a testament to painful accommodation. Hard choices are about forgoing something you really need for something else you really need, only worse. There are always blood, guts and abandoned music lessons oozing between the line items. Every good budget is a poignant memorial to deserving deeds left undone. The operative term is *sacrifice*. But then, working people know this intuitively. While the privileged, increasingly the sole guardians of our national treasury, lack this penny-wise prowess. Vast personal wealth can undo the most earnest attempts at conservatism.

Our current inherited rich guy has been an abysmal steward of the nation's fiscal well-being. True to ill-formed character and social position, George II did not hash out a budget. He offered up a self-indulgent wish-list gilded by the usual paper tigers: a money press, an *e pluribus unum* stamp, and a lifetime of privilege. Our grandchildren are now on the hook for a mortgage more onerous than JFK I's worst imaginings. If he cringed at mortgaged digs, what would Kennedy make of loans leveraged on the backs of entire future generations? Though it falls from a greater height, even a rich guy's penny drops one day.

ALL THE WORLD'S A PHASE

"...the American publisher's argument for truncation was based on a conviction that the original version, showing as it does a capacity for regeneration in even the most depraved soul, was a kind of capitulation to the British Pelagian spirit, whereas the Augustinian Americans were tough enough to accept an image of unregenerable man.. I was in no position to protest, except feebly and in the expectation of being overborne: I needed the couple of hundred dollars that comprised the advance on the work."—Anthony Burgess, from 'A Clockwork Orange: A play with music'

Maybe we shouldn't be too hard on the Democrats. America's Augustinians have vanquished more formidable opponents than the befuddled donkey. Take Anthony Burgess, for example. In the above quote, Burgess explains his acquiescence to excising the final chapter of *A Clockwork Orange* from the American edition. When we last left you dear reader, this chapter had Alex admitting to his youthful indiscretions and planning for an uneventful adulthood. And so there it was, raked, bundled, all so neat and tidy like a well-tended English garden. Opting in this instance for the sunnier side of his lifelong preoccupation with good-versus-evil, Burgess regenerates Alex in the best tradition of British Pelagianism. But to the American publisher's sensibility, this was a too-cheery resolution, perfunctorily redemptive in tone. After all, the electric chair was invented for the likes of Alex. So why not use it on the little git? Should man's vengeance overreach, God is there to sort the confusion on the other side, or so St. Augustine might say.

A cognitive behaviorist, George Lakoff proposes his own secularized bipolarity in *Moral Politics: How Liberals and Conservatives Think* and its synopsized version, *Don't Think of an Elephant: Know Your Values and Frame the Debate* (the latter being a sort of 2004 electioneering handbook for erstwhile Democrats.) Reading both, I was immediately struck by the parallels to Burgessian dualism. For those that haven't, I urge them to read *The Wanting Seed* for the most complete treatment of his Pelagian/Augustinian cycle. To paraphrase here, Burgess argues that societies continually veer between two extremes. First, there is the permissive Pelagian phase, named after the fifth century British monk who drove St. Augustine to distraction with the audacious notion of man's perfectibility. During this period, society basks in the inherent goodness of mankind.

It's a wondrous, magical time when floral motifs abound and people slip daisy stems into gun barrels. Then, just when it seems geraniums have forever trumped gulags, a growing licentiousness threatens the social order. Security concerns eclipse libertarian prerogatives. Emboldened during the pendulum's reactive arc, Augustinians find their true vocation as storm troopers. Himmleresque Attorneys General rise to power. Patriot Acts pass with virtual unanimity. Flower power withers on the vine. The periods between these two extremes, Burgess called 'interphases'. During these interphases, society, sensing it has veered off in one direction, takes steps to reclaim the happy middle. But where Burgess merely consigns us to a perpetual sine wave, Lakoff is out to steal all our fun. For Lakoff, we are yesterday's Red Barons in an auto-pilot world, hopelessly shackled to one of two determinative orientations: the stern father or the nurturant parent. Rather fortuitously, these 'cognitive frames' acquit to conservative and liberal, Republican and Democrat.

In the deep, dark recesses of his cognitive framework, Lakoff is a full-blown Augustinian. For him, politics is something like Original Sin meeting *The Manchurian Candidate*. Not only are we yoked to our frames (a sort of secular predestinarianism), we're shockingly susceptible to well-crafted language cues. Lakoff, clearly a Grover-Norquist-of-the-left aspirant, suggests Republican excite their base with just the right cognitive pillow-talk, whereas Democrats are forever stumbling into carefully set linguistic traps. Fox News is particularly adept at these frame-ups, lobbing patently unfair questions at their 'fair and balanced' panelists. For example, the Democratic pundit is an a priori goner in a debate over 'tax relief'. The term itself is deftly skewed since 'relief' implies alleviation of an inordinately unfair burden. Thus Republicans manage to sidestep honest debate on a very controversial topic.

The 'death tax' is another cognitively-charged bit of business. Surely taxing someone for dying is the fiscal equivalent of desecrating graves. Never mind that the tax is on the estate, and not the deceased. Once again, Democrats are left to dance atop the head of an extracted hand grenade pin. Lakoff employs this Democrat/Pelagian argument relentlessly. For anyone who has ever asked themselves 'why the hell are we even talking about this', Lakoff's body of inquiry is a fascinating examination of the manipulations perpetrated by politicians of all stripes on a malleable electorate. However Lakoff is at his best when he's a non-aligned cognitive behaviorist and not the Democratic Party's First Cheerleader. According to Lakoff, seventy per cent of us are roughly divided between the two dominant frames. The remaining third sort of flap in the wind (cognitively speaking) and are the real sought-after prize in the ongoing battle of ideas. This merry band of loose cannons is often referred to as the 'swing vote'. Without these bird-brains forever tipping elections in one direction or another, Lakoff's scheme would never get its Burgessian wings.

Lakoff's prescription is clear, if shamelessly derivative: Democrats must become more like Republicans. But is there a fly on this elephant? Historically, Democrats have prided themselves on their role as the rallying point of a chorus of the dispossessed. This house of many voices is at odds with a top-down executive summary. Thus Lakoff seems to put the Democrats on the horns of a cognitive dilemma: how to distill their multicultural interests into a lean, mean talking machine.

As if to inspire the troops, Lakoff points out the Republicans' similar disarray and intra-party rancor during the 1950's. Despite

Goldwater's abysmal showing in the 1964 Presidential election, Lakoff points out, the Arizonan's very presence on the ballot becomes the first real conservative victory in what would mark a string of victories extending, with remarkable consistency, to the present-day. Another seminal event was soon-to-be Supreme Court Justice Lewis Powell's famous 1970 letter where he urged conservative forces to establish a more assertive presence on universities for the purpose of winning over young minds gone soft on a diet of anti-establishment propaganda. This initiative helped launch conservative think tanks such as the Heritage Foundation. In relative short order, disparate conservative interests began reaping the rewards of a movement where 'everyone pushed together'.

The message to the current crop of bickering Democrats: it can be done. But it will take courage and discipline, attributes the Democrats do not currently possess in great abundance. The truth is, Democrats in the wake of 9/11 painted themselves into a dithering corner, dealing the cause of nurturance a grievous blow. An aroused mother bear is possibly nature's best example of how nurturance and a spirited defense of the homeland need not be mutually exclusive. It pays to remember that Woodrow Wilson, FDR and Harry Truman—Democrats all—were the Nervous Nellies who navigated us through two world wars.

It would be instructive to ask Messrs. Bush and Cheney how they felt with LBJ at the helm during their Vietnam service were it not for the fact that both mens' service records are in varying states of MIA. Incipient fascists will insist that nurturance can be indulged only when the nest is properly secured from predation. Furthermore, this moment in history cries out for manly men; certainly a convenient enough argument for relegating Lakoff and his folks to a position of perpetual loyal opposition during times of grave danger to the homeland, real or perceived. Indeed the crucial swing votes swung hard for Papa George. Augustinian Americans everywhere were suddenly claiming, smugly, that America had always been a right-of-center nation anyway, and that the Democrats had misunderstood the country all along. Too bad Burgess isn't here. He'd assure us it's a passing phase.

The Democrats have done themselves no recent favors. Just when the cause of liberty needed the do-or-die exuberance of a Patrick Henry, the only taker in the Senate was Russ Feingold—the one dissenting Senatorial vote against the Patriot Act. He should be applauded both for his courage and his speed-reading skills. The cause of liberty always suffers from an abundance of well-wishers during fat times, and a shortage of champions when its existence is imperiled.

Whether one believes we are victims of opportunistic fear-mongering or that Islamic nihilists are 'unregenerable men' with a death-wish, the Democrats might have laid better claim to equal-parent status with a countervailing voice of reason amidst the post-9/11 clamor, arguably hysteria, for security-at-all-costs. As it is, they ducked and pulled a domestic Tonkin resolution. That will be the historical explanation anyway, the way we explain the cycle's current permutation. The fact is Pelagians are pariahs in the Age of Terror. And so, faced with an exogenous terror threat, the fulcrum of popular sentiment that serves, in a free society, to militate between the conflicting desires for security and liberty tilted decisively in the direction of the former. Whether, in the aftermath of 9/11, we succumbed to cynical manipulation or were the beneficiaries of firm, decisive leadership is, Lakoff might suggest, a matter of cognitive interpretation. For now George Bush, our stern-father-of-the-moment, has delivered us squarely into an Augustinian age. Let's hope Burgess was right, and the pendulum finds its way back to center.

ONE NATION, UNDER WHOSE GOD?

"I trust God speaks through me. Without that, I couldn't do my job."—George Bush addressing an Amish group (as reported in the Lancaster New Era, July 16, 2004)

A social libertarian, I normally avoid judging other people's religious beliefs. Until the revival tent comes to Washington, that is. Then all reticence can take a hike. The product of a buttoned-down, under-sexed Calvinist upbringing, I was raised to believe banking and religion, properly practiced, shared one crucial similarity: they were boring as hell. Any sense of drama or—God forbid—fun was a portent of looming disaster. This heavy-on-the-starch moral restraint is at odds with the Pentecostals' penchant for pyrotechnic hyperbole. There's just no appetite in the Lone Star State for stiff-backed Yankee rectitude. Free beer, wild-catting, fire and brimstone are what pass for a quiet day in Texas. But there I go judging again.

Let me add that I share with many Christians their despondency over the coarsening of this nation's cultural life and the general trashing of the polis. So the impulse to wash everyone's mouths out with soap is hardly foreign to me. If I read the New Testament and St. Augustine correctly, part of the Christian's burden is to shuffle through this mortal coil, holding his nose mostly. But even a good ascetic can snap. When Christians shed their meekness and assume the reins of power, the theocratic impulse often overwhelms them. Cowboys make especially lousy doormats.

Then there are the prophetic self-fulfillers, who are looking not only for a good fight, but for The Fight. Perhaps I speak from the agony of effeteness, but when a president's foreign policy toolbox includes Armageddon and the Antichrist, I want to sequester the red phone. Who knows, George Bush may hanker for hell-on-earth as a necessary prelude to ushering in God's Kingdom. Presidents once gave the appearance of working diligently to avert the Great Conflagration: Containment over Calvary, that was the ticket. I suppose I preferred presidents who were Christian to Christian presidents. Where are the Methodists when we need them? John Kennedy's detractors feared he would consult the Vatican on matters of state. However a good fundamentalist brooks no earthly intercessors. When God has his ear, it's usually with a vengeance.

Surely Ayn Rand would read this administration very darkly. For her, faith and reason were inextricably linked in a zero-sum game. More of one invariably meant less of the other, with tyranny and illegitimate force flourishing in a climate of out-sized faith. The Iraq War is George Bush's most disastrous faith-based initiative. Not surprisingly, the explicit 'reasons' for Iraq have eluded most thoughtful commentators.

But I want to afford religion every consideration. Speaking in ancient Semitic tongues while under the Holy Spirits' watchful eye is a venerable American pastime. Even rattlesnake handling has a place at the Great Table so long as the serpents aren't housed on government property. This is the essence of church-state separation. But how does an individual psyche, heavily colored by an apocalyptic theme, partition itself effectively? Does the Pit of Fire countenance firewalls? When is a president, even in his quiet contemplative moments, not mere seconds away from 'having to be president' again? With all this ducking back and forth between Superman and Clark Kent, might George Bush catch his cape in the phone booth door?

What people choose to do behind closed doors with their rattlesnakes is a private affair. Of infinitely more concern are the geopolitical pretensions of Christian fundamentalism, specifically its life-negating aspirations—if that's not too oxymoronic. This prophecy business can easily spiral into eerie self-fulfillment. If Bush feels he is a prophesied figure (in fairness, I don't know that he does), then his recent 'mandate' can only add fuel to the Pit of Fire. Middle East conflagration? No problem. Everything's falling into place. With the world teetering toward hell-in-a-hand-basket, the Christian fundamentalists are beside themselves with...rapture. This should send reasonable people (many Christians counted among them) into prayerful conniptions.

As many of us labor in the here-and-now with conscientious conviction, others may be instigating conflict, urging the universe to 'bring it on' (to quote a recent Bushism.) Suffice to say there is, within the end-times crowd, a disturbing acquiescence to calamity. I would call it a death-wish, a Jungian shadow-manifestation. Perversely, the Born Again's call it a 'culture of life'. Texas' death-row inmates don't know what to make of this debate, so they stick to marking their calendars, day by day, and filing appeals.

If there are autonomously functioning civic and religious George Bushes, the man has done little to demarcate the line publicly. Indeed he seems to thrive on the margin with winks and nods to the amen chorus. This is a White House famous for its prayer-circling and Bible study. Dr. Jack van Impe, who never met a current affair he couldn't biblically implicate, has found a sympathetic ear in the Bush administration. For all we know, George Bush may have stumbled across himself in some obscure Old Testament passage. More ominous still, some good soul on the Internet has discovered that, when you sum the letters in George Bush's name, multiply by the square root of the Carlyle Group's net income and divide by pi, the result is 666. This good versus evil thing can get very bizarre, very fast.

My own hunch is that the overt religiosity displayed by the public man is real—which only makes it more alarming. I'd sleep better knowing there was a calculating, Dick Nixon at the helm. Now there was a paranoia you could trust. At least deviousness operates within the normal—albeit seedier—realms of reason. Vote counters are eminently reachable. So yes, it's okay to wax nostalgic for the carnal, earthbound antics of Bill Clinton. Though he perhaps navigated with a certain moral ambivalence, Clinton was a master at altering course. As most managerial text books will attest, pragmatic flexibility is not a bad trait in a CEO.

By contrast, Bush supporters speak glowingly of their Leader's 'unswervingness'. The worse things get, the more he feels he is simply being 'tested'. When guided by the hand of God, there are no false paths, only demonic attempts to derail one's righteous journey. This is analogous to the downhill skier who, losing his footing, careens down the mountain smashing into numerous pylons. His most avid fans assure us he is simply testing his body. Others say he is falling. Bush embraces the stubborn constancy of Job. But self-correcting resourcefulness, as any fan of *The Simpsons* will tell you, gets Homer out of a lot of tough scrapes.

Behind every public saint, there must be a scrupulously attendant sinner. Karl Rove is the embodiment of everything George Bush can't bring himself to stoop to, and yet needs for political viability. The old man had Lee 'Willie Horton' Atwater, missing him desperately in the 1992 election. A political animal, Rove has his feet firmly planted in the Earthly City. Moreover he wields Bush's faith to maximum political effect. The morality issue that dominated the last election was Rove's subliminal clarion call, alerting the faithful to the rising tide of anti-Christian forces everywhere: Islamic fundamentalists abroad and uppity homosexual 'unionists' at home. In the perpetual looming shadow of apocalypse, traditional public policy issues suddenly become *de minimus* unless they can be shown to have a direct bearing on the disposition of the soul. It's pointless really, bemoaning budget deficits, Social Security, and jobs when the sky's about to explode into a tabernacle of singing angels. Meanwhile Halliburton laughs all the way to the Gulf. Quite brilliant, really.

The English are not a particularly religious people. So perhaps *The Daily Mirror* can be excused for its post-election headline "How Can 59,054,087 People Be So Dumb?" Well into what appears—on the Continent at least—to be the post-Christian era (or as the Pope, with plaintive optimism, chooses to characterize it, Europe's current 'waywardness'), Europeans regard Bush's re-election with incredulity. After all, it defies all logic and reason. Indeed it does. Bush's re-election requires a sort of supra-rational analysis because it is, at least in part, transcendentally derived. To those still yoked to the secularist claptrap about 'passing along a better planet to successive generations', well, you're all just irreligious farts anyway. Never mind that the betterment of life on Earth has venerable—and stubborn—Christian roots dating back to the Pelagian heresy. It's Satan, at his diversionary best, who compels so many to strive towards making the world a better place. The message is clear: engage the world and imperil your soul; imperil the world and your soul ascends.

BIG GOVERNMENT AND THE BIG EASY

"...each proposal must be weighed in the light of...the need to maintain balance between the private and the public economy;"—from President Dwight D. Eisenhower's "Military-Industrial Complex" speech, 1961

New Orleans languishes today in a state of economic disrepair. With disruptions to the normal balance of life so complete, the traditional paths to economic recovery—aid, grants, job programs, private charities—cannot take hold. The self-healing, virtuous circle has been severed: no jobs, no people, no people, no jobs. When economic activity comes to a dead stop, what or whom steps in as the Prime Mover?

America is a nation of near-boundless resources. The material needs posed by New Orleans's plight are eminently surmountable. Given the abysmal public sector response to Katrina's aftermath, the question begs asking: Does this country's leadership still possess the ingredients of character to make possible today what it accomplished for other nations fifty years ago?

Indeed an example exists in recent American history that dwarfs New Orleans in every logistical metric. The manifold challenges posed by WWII and its aftermath ushered in a golden age of public service in America. Intent on doing whatever was needed to secure the larger effort, the best and the brightest gravitated towards government. Money was an afterthought. Greed was still a deadly sin, hardly an ethos. This public spirit was put to the test again rebuilding a ravaged Europe at war's end. America faced the New Orleans' catch-22, but on a vaster scale. Yet the question was the same: how does a society rescue its traumatized economy from the death-spiral of low employment and profoundly disrupted supply?

Summarizing Dean Acheson's watershed foreign policy speech of May 1947, David McCullough, in his biography *Truman*, says this:

> "The stricken countries of Europe needed everything and could afford to buy nothing. Financial aid was imperative, but, as Acheson stressed, the objective was not relief, it was the revival of industry, agriculture and trade."

This was market-making of the highest order. Nothing of its magnitude had ever been attempted before. Exceeding even the revolutionary era (forever besmirched by the stain of slavery), the nation has never been endowed with such an array of morally sound men. George Marshall, Harry Truman, Dean Acheson, George Kennan and Dwight Eisenhower threw themselves into winning the peace with the same intensity displayed during the war. Realizing the private sector lacked the resources to launch products *and* markets with crucial simultaneity these gray-haired titans of public service crafted the Marshall Plan, or as it was formally known, the European Recovery Program.

This effort, combined with the two pillars of post-war entitlement, the GI Bill and the VA Loan, got the world back to business in a hurry. The government's central role was soon forgotten in the mad dash to prosperity. How forgotten? Today it's fashionable for the beneficiaries of this massive public sector initiative to rail against the evils of meddlesome government.

The Republican Party, chafing at the massive $17 billion price tag, opposed the Marshall Plan initially. But then, so did the Left, specifically the American Progressive and the American Communist parties. Traditionally, when a fundamental imperative looms large in America, there is a pragmatic strain that rises up, dispatching ideological purists. For a number of reasons, ideological exactitude lends itself more to intellectualized, perhaps even effete, European politics. In their heart of hearts, Americans subscribe to common sense. After hard lobbying from Truman, the Marshall Plan passed with near-unanimity in 1948.

Political parties are loath to champion a hero outside their own ranks. Thus neither Right nor Left is prone to recite the following ideological inconvenience: the America government was the unabashed hero of the WWII era. Neither the industrial class, nor the American proletariat (such as it is) alone could have triumphed over fascism. In a sterling example of the whole exceeding the sum of its parts, the system of arrangement, the governing principle i.e. the government itself provided the crucial element for success. So a belated 'hurray' for government.

Captains of industry are not renowned for their generosity of spirit. Sharing credit, especially with the public sector, is tantamount to requesting a boost in the corporate income tax rate. But the fact is the profit motive owes its motive force to an *a priori* climate of relative stability. Stated another way, business thrives in, but hardly creates, the polis. Good governance is thus a necessity for profitable enterprise. Yes Virginia, business needs government more than government needs business. For anyone doubting the order of this sequence, go visit Haiti.

Perhaps America's moral climate—reflected undeniably in its public spirit—wavered in the ensuing fat years of prosperity. Thirty years after the Marshall Plan, Ronald Reagan, former GE pitchman, would build a legacy on besmirching the public sector. The consummate shill, Reagan delivered his free market devotionals with cue-card discipline—and 3x5 vacuities. As to whether his pitch was ever vetted for reality, well, veracity is hardly the first-order concern of a carnival barker. In fact listening to Reagan, one might easily have concluded it was the free market—and not the free world led by free governments—that averted global totalitarianism.

On the contrary, Big business is highly adaptable, getting along famously with liberal democrats and fascists alike. Though it was Eisenhower who would coin the term in later years, a military-industrial complex fueled the Nazi war effort; companies with exotic names like Ford, GM and ITT. Sound familiar? Yes, they were our war profiteers too. No sticklers on points of ideology, many venerable companies worked double-duty. With both sides needing bullets, industry was often spared the task of choosing sides. Flesh-and-blood public servants, raised to salute in one direction, were not so fortunate.

Nobody has ever been pulled from a burning building by a corporation. And yet, there is a certain school of thought that argues today's corporations are big fuzzy citizens with feelings too. Of course this is the same school that believes New Improved Tide has perfected whiter whites. Yahoo and Microsoft, 'progressive' companies claiming 21st century new paradigms, routinely hand over search information to the Chinese government. For this, people are jailed, perhaps even killed. Offering arrogance as a defense, these companies aver that China is a big market. Whew, thanks for clearing *that* up. They also admit, in so many words, that civil rights are not really their business; software is. After the left-hand-right-hand shenanigans of WWII, no one should be surprised at the amorality of the bottom-line-seekers. The question is do we want an implicitly unprincipled force to be the organizing principle for our society, Walmart government at unbeatably low prices?

Today's corporations, no different from yesterday's corporations, would have America's kids back in coal-mines tomorrow if not for those persnickety child labor laws. Yet there is a plaintive echo of American exceptionalism in the notion that American children will never again suffer the plight of nine-year-old rug-makers in Lahore. After all, this country has 'evolved' through its progressive era. Upton Sinclair exposed the meat-packers. The muckrakers prevailed. Had there been something intrinsically sacrosanct about America, surely our industrial base would have clung to the heartland in a determined effort to make things work. Instead they headed off-shore to countries where labor activism looms in a very distant future. Progressive victories are reversible. Remove government and Junior would be jack-hammering igneous rock formations faster than you could say 'adolescent black lung'.

This is not a treatise for industrial policy or democratic socialism.

Most of us would settle for such rudimentary prohibitions as no lead in our drinking water. Gulp. It's just that those pastoral ADM advertisements should be taken with a grain of salt. Corporations are still the best little whorehouses in Texas. Their anti-social tendencies must be reined in to better serve the public good. Government is the only entity capable of doing this.

So exactly what type of system do the corporatists have in mind for us? By this essayist's reckoning, George Bush Senior's thousand points of light worked out to approximately one sixty-watt bulb for every 300,000 citizens. By design, old George's 'points' were to be kept in a state of perpetual disconnect; in short, no organizing principle, no power-sharing grid, no Marshall Plan. This metaphor of patchy luminosity offers a glimpse into the corporatist agenda: Isolate the heroes and avert a national movement. Should the heroes die, as heroes often do, thousands fall back into the inky blackness where they're easier to control. The abrupt and mysterious demise of firebrands such as Huey Long and Karen Silkwood suggests that something in the American ethos is hazardous to the health of populists.

In the current era of private sector blow-ups and rapacious greed ala Enron and Worldcom, Reagan's disparaging typecast of the 'lazy, bumbling public servant' (sad corollary to his mythic welfare queen), becomes all the more scurrilous for its unanswered character assassination. Reagan's cynical renderings of the typical public servant made the despairing assertion that, if people are not working for obscene sums of money, then they couldn't possibly be working at all. But we call too-large sums of money obscene for a reason. The suggestion here is that honest labor is not an innate expression of man, but rather something he barters up, always with a jealous eye cast to the bottom-line. This sounds like meretricious self-servitude, man counting himself out like so many pieces of gold. For many, some of the best things in life are done for free, without compunction, without monetary incentive.

Equally ludicrous is the idea that, faced with the opportunity of making just $30 million a day instead of, say, $40 million a day, Bill Gates would slip into such a dispirited funk that he'd stop creating software engineering jobs for kids in India. So please, no tax increases for the poor rich.

'Man-as-economic-automaton' theories tend to denigrate the preponderance of human endeavor over the ages, lashing them all to a Form W-2. Before Bill Gates ever thought to build a 60,000 square foot home, he was a human stew of passion, incentive and drive. Marginal tax rates did little to encourage—or dissuade—him from doing what he appears to do exceedingly well. After achieving their subsistence needs, people, the worthwhile ones anyway, work for passion not money. To say otherwise strips the humanity from human achievement. As many a starving artist will attest, there is much more to human aspiration than the mercenary impulse. Only a shill withholds speech for remuneration.

At this point, Thomas Paine or Patrick Henry might chime in, 'we made free speech free for a reason. Some of us answer to the ultimate employer, our conscience.' Light-years away from Reagan-Bush corporatism, this stubbornly inalienable aspect of free speech still strikes some folks as the quintessence of America. After all, what did our brave public servants fight and die for? The right to speak in the public square or Ronald Reagan's right, as paid spokesman, to denigrate public sacrifice while extolling the virtues of GE? Even in this era of GE-underwritten broadcast 'journalism', we must hope there's still a difference.

As Reagan served his country during WWII in the crucial role of thespian, risking rashes from face-paint, it's possible the more perilous and singularly unprofitable contributions made by others in the war effort were entirely lost on him. Or, as a supply-sider might point out, dying for ones country all but guarantees a precipitous fall-off in lifetime earnings. Such is the economic calamity that awaits public servants called upon to make the ultimate public sacrifice. In another time, we called them patriots.

When the National Anthem plays, micro-economists should remove their green-eye shades and avert their gazes in respectful silence. Defying profit motives, rational expectations and wealth-maximization theories, thousands of people who gave their lives in WWII were essentially broke. Yet heroism is not a venerable smokescreen for economic ineptitude...right?

How else to explain why the greatest contributors to our culture and civilization, gifted men and women, routinely die in abject poverty? Perhaps they received horrible estate planning advice. Perhaps they saw beyond wealth and power, poor bastards.

Produce a private sector resume that boasts the equivalent of The Marshall Plan, The Manhattan Project, The Interstate Highway System and the Apollo Program, and this peon to public sector accomplishment will be abandoned forthwith. Think of that apocryphal moment in American achievement when a bunch of government bureaucrats navigated a near-inoperable Apollo 13 safely back to Earth. It's hard to recall a private sector accomplishment that rivals this moment of quintessential American genius. Stock options can only gnash their teeth enviously. Some pages from history demolish the best right-wing polemics.

One triumph of the Reaganite disinformation campaign is that being 'for government' enjoys all the public cache of root canals. Even the Democrats have been cowed. No one champions public service anymore. This is hardly an appeal for government-of-a-million-paper-cuts or the stultifying omnipresence of a Big Brother involved in all things great and small. The Orwellian objections to Big Government are certainly valid and may yet come to pass. Yes, government-led fascism is something to be feared. But corporate fascism, with a quiescent government in tow, is every bit as oppressive. And it's what we have now.

Rather, this is a tribute to the grand gesture, the noble human endeavor of monumental scale. It is the recognition that government, when allowed to think big, can tackle truly Big Things. Today's government is overrun by small men with small ideas, custodians of narrow private interests, who are bought and paid for with private dollars. From these men, any pretense towards public service, in the time-honored sense of that calling, is a smokescreen for something decidedly less seemly. Follow the money trail to chart the animating principle of their public fervors.

Like Dresden after the war, the Big Easy is a big need awaiting a grand gesture. In a prior time, Marshall and Eisenhower would have seized the moment. As it is, the city awaits a public sector largesse and commitment that may belong to a bygone era. One wonders whether the city suffers further disadvantage since it beckons from within. Power, particularly in its current permutation, insists on staring outward, in search of fresh new axes of evil. Because New Orleans is in America, it's like a discarded lover, long since conquered, seduced and subdued. FEMA would do well to take a lesson from Hezbollah who wasted no time distributing charity at home.

Instead, our leaders appear bored at the prospect of swabbing the decks of the Big Easy. After all, New Orleans is a national embarrassment in which no vainglorious war-hawk wishes to be caught dead. The photo ops are horrible. These guys live to exude power; not wade, ankle-deep, in muck and pathos.

So that's where we are. Short of blowing things up, it's impolitic today to be seen exhibiting much proficiency in government. As J. Edgar Hoover might opine, a too-hearty appetite for public service has the smell of communism or worse, flagrant homosexuality.

George Marshall was as brilliant and committed in peace as he was in war; from Army Chief of Staff during WWII to Secretary of State in his 'second career' as diplomat. Reagan's heirs, by contrast, must always be seen to be bristling under their public mantles. After all, they inhabit a role they're ideologically on record as detesting: "Service? We came to town for power. In order to retain power, we must dismantle service." That is the weird two-step the Republicans dance to time and again. They are the great dismantlers, the barbarians within the gates. Pure poison to the notion of honorable governance, they find the term itself an oxymoron.

If character is forbearance, few of us can claim the character of an Eisenhower. Weary veteran of the inglorious realities of war, Ike knew instinctively that a myriad of terrible toys stored up in a Pentagon warehouse was an accident waiting to happen. Some loopy cowboy was someday bound to stumble into hand's reach of the red phone.

The high art of bloodless posturing and symbolic 'shows of force', really what a superpower does best, would eventually overwhelm a smaller man's sense of inadequacy. An escalation into very big bangs was practically ensured; bangs the country might not recover from. For an untested male, the inevitable use of force can be like the first law of testosterone, as immutable as physics itself. Let's try this stuff out. There isn't a weapon that's never been used. President Eisenhower had nothing to prove. Bush, by fifty, had little to show. So the gun just went off in his hand.

Think of the classroom bully (often the covert classroom coward) who must wear a halo for the school play. He does so only because his parents promise him a new bike if he plays nice. That's what public service has become in the hands of the Reaganites. Their namesake played an unconscionable role in the assault on public service. Surely Eisenhower, a warrior of deeds, would have seen Reagan and his ilk coming. Judging from the cautionary tone of Ike's last presidential speech, perhaps he did.

There is plenty of blame to go around; Reagan for hoodwinking us, GE for incubating his glibness. But most of all, the shame is ours for ignoring the innumerable examples that contradicted the Gipper's shallow diatribes.

This then has been a tribute to the manifold blessings of good government which, in the final analysis, can only be underwritten by a decent people. May history grant us the good fortune to enjoy good governance again. Until then, the Big Easy waits in an uneasy shambles.

THE BUSH WHACKING THE DOG

Watching the tear-stained face of our great leader as he posthumously awarded Navy SEAL Michael Monsoor a Medal of Honor yesterday, I came away haunted by Bush's final quote to the young man's parents "America owes you a debt that can never be repaid." As though the books aren't cooked enough. This so-called debt—denominated in steadily mounting American casualties—has so far eluded all sane attempts at calculation. How can America begin to repay a debt that it cannot first explain to itself?

It would shame me to think I was besmirching Michael Monsoor's unassailable bravery. In fact I am in awe at what he did. So much so that I can't help but decry the utter squandering of his noble attributes. I would only note that character of the nature displayed springs from a personal arsenal that is largely impervious to the contextual merits of its expression. Toss a brave man into a unmitigated disaster and you can be assured of one thing: he will conduct himself the only way his nature allows, with selfless courage and valor. This says nothing of the disaster or its architects, though I find the public tears an affront (if not a contrived front) that work only to cloud the Chief Architect's complicity.

The better question is, how did a young man of such sterling character find himself in a war of such dubious merit? It's for the annals of valor now that, by throwing himself on a hand grenade, this young man saved the lives of his comrades. But I feel we should be less celebratory of the sacrifice as aghast at the senseless loss. We could have used a man like that in a long productive life here at home. Perhaps even as President. Thus the question is begged: Why was such a man—and those whose lives he saved—even there in the first place? To call this an utterly needless tale of heroism does nothing to diminish the heroic act itself. At least, I intend to proceed with that distinction firmly in mind.

It's becoming my tired narcissist tract, but surely we didn't ransack an entire region so that Americans could display personal tales of unparalleled bravery? Or did we? Is this 'be all that you can be' run amuck, at the cost of innumerable women and children who no longer 'are' so that we could more fully 'be'? If so, then I have grossly underestimated the grip of our narcissist affliction. Bush said recently he envied the excitement and sense of romance our young people must feel fighting in this great cause. Romance? Beginning with Matthew Brady's Civil War photography and continuing through All Quiet on the Western Front, romance has been purged from the war-lexicon of thoughtful human beings everywhere. Despite its complete discrediting in serious-minded circles, the romance of war lingered on for awhile as a bankable Hollywood conceit. But even the movies had gotten hip to the beat by the late seventies with such bleak fare as *The Deer Hunter* and *Apocalypse Now*. That war is a pointless hell has become virtually pabulum in all quarters.

So I cringe at the mindset, echoed in the Bush persona, that depicts, for example, John Wayne as a 'great American'. Not content simply to be a swaggering thespian of such peacetime nonentities as *Reap the Wild Wind* and *The Shepherd of the Hills*, Wayne was a war propagandist, an on-camera Leni Riefenstahl. One could ask, rhetorically, by how many days the ludicrous vainglory of *The Green Berets* prolonged the Vietnam debacle, even coaxed additional young Americans to 'serve their country', perhaps to die? Hero? John Wayne had a make-up man, for christsakes. His vocation, rooted in deception (the benign term is 'make-believe'), called on him to wear ketchup-splattered costumes, the better to perpetuate the deadliest of spells.

My best dime store psychoanalysis, worth exactly what you pay for it, is that Bush envies the WW II war record of his highly-decorated father (himself a brave young man by any reckoning). Consequently, he bears an existential burden of shame at his own failure to seize his 'romantic interlude' in Vietnam—dare I say a case of impotence sulking in the generational shadow of omnipotence? Moreover as Chief Decider (a rather impetuous self-image suggesting junior in dad's clothes), he has been permitted to indulge a dangerous vicariousness on the backs of our brave young men and women who are cut it seems from a similar cloth to Bush Senior—if not alas from the same direct lineage. No matter how many bogus aircraft carrier landings are put-on for this petulant prodigal son, the shame will never be erased. The debt will never be assuaged. Terribly sorry, luv ya, buh-bye.

This is not to say that there are not yet countless more brave young Americans, oblivious to this Oedipal subtext, ready to perform in an heroic manner (It's a tautology. How else *can* they perform?) But what a shameful misappropriation of youth and personal valor. And what about that dragged-along realm beyond our shores, the world *over there,* perennial rubber room to our ill-conceived adventures? Surely it tires of our forward-march-damn-the-torpedoes mentality, not to mention our chronic tendency to mistake the sensible counsel of traditional friends and allies for incoming torpedoes.

Speaking of the world, it is too often conducted by cowards, those who aspire to control and array others in the hopes of better safeguarding their own hides. Who else would want the leadership gig as a regular mainstay? There is no amount of brave blood that will quench them of their self-doubts. In the end, character, even of the substandard variety, cannot wash out. By a similar calculus, no cost—born especially as it is by others—is too great to those who excel above all else at camouflaging their weakness. Bush hasn't 'cured' his early cowardice. He has advanced it, calamitously, onto the world stage. Furthermore he is far too much the coward to send others into retreat. His legendary intransigence is a facet of paralytic fear. The painful process of moving America forward cannot begin until Bush is moved to the side.

ON THE RECENT FREE SPEECH FLAP, IMUS CONFESS MY RESERVATIONS

Truth be told (and who better to truth-tell than a spin-free polemicist?) few people really care for the loud, variegated din that is free speech. That would be like championing brussel sprouts. Of course they'll cheer for their own team. That's like championing ice cream. Free speech—the kind in need of protecting anyway—is not the ugly stepmother's sycophantic mirror parroting narcissistic bromides. We've already had the *Stepford Wives* remake and frankly it sucked. No, in its fullest permutation (and how else to broach constitutionality but in its totality, warts and all?) free speech is an ugly spectacle. If you're liking everything you hear, then it probably ain't free speech anymore. It's Disneyland, or Ambien country. Controversiality is the dialectic that sparks robust debate. A society that worships calm courts the worst form of inarticulateness.

I suspect we're out of practice talking to one another. That's one reason America's national debates always end up careening down false trails. Our native ability to render uncoaxed, free speech has atrophied from an over-proliferation of transmit-only commercial venues. There we are, mute and ears cocked, to the nearest 'telling device'. Has the couch finally rocked our potato-heads to sleep?

With so much money in the temple one can be forgiven, I suppose, for mistaking the pigs for the men. However after this essay, I won't forgive you for letting it happen again. Imus' 'speech' was not free speech at all, but commercial speech, bought and paid for by a series of sponsors who derived economic advantage from his ability to draw an audience. In this context, the mechanics of commercial speech worked just as Adam Smith's invisible-hand-in-fast-retreat should. Pressured by their customer base these sponsors made a quick back-of-the-envelope calculation and decided that the cost-benefit had tipped against this particular promotional tool and that it was time to plow more cash into billboards and scantily-clad dancing girls (or at least let's hope). At the end of the day and despite what he may have thought of himself, Imus was a tool to sell soap. Draping the discussion in constitutional language is more than a bit high-falutin. Imus is free to spout his views on the street corner, though I would urge him to avoid Harlem's 125th Street for all the obvious reasons.

There's no tinnier sound than when a grown corporation cries. CBS chairman Les Moonves' press release announcing Imus' firing was a doozie (a scolding that took a full eight days to congeal into a 'statement'.) Had he been an indefatigable commercial speech spokesman (and why apologize for capitalism?) Moonves should have said—"We are a bloodless, asocial entity known as a corporation. The profit motive has evaporated beneath our feet. Imus is gone." Hey man, I sell soap and this gig ain't workin' for us anymore. See ya. This debate doesn't warrant Jeffersonian pretensions. Though people do love reaching for the powdered wigs.

One of the great advantages of commercial speech (among myriad disadvantages) is that in most instances it can be turned off by the offended party like a spigot—with the spin of a radio dial or the click of a TV remote control. Perhaps it's the growth of secondary media outlets like Youtube that compels folks—who normally would not be listening to Imus anyway—to 'tune in for a sampling of the offense'. Thus the sense of outrage cascades well beyond Imus' naturally inclined audience. One gets the feeling the various resentment classes—certainly their shepherds—stand ready to mobilize their flocks at the first sign of crude remarks. For example, rather than compound the hurt by propagating the comments out to folks who wouldn't encounter them under normal circumstances, why not shield the unoffended? Why lead them to the very diatribe where their feelings are sure to be hurt and their self-esteem injured? This is not the next door neighbor standing at the fence-line spewing obscenities about your wife. Depending on what you think of your wife that could be a real problem. No, there is a rehearsed nature to the press-conference outrage that belies the very notion of rage.

Are people seeking offense for self-validation? I heard someone complain recently about the saturation coverage surrounding Anna Nicole Smith's death. Every station seemed to be regurgitating the same footage, he said. My suggestion, sacrilegious to be sure, was to turn the TV off. Read a book. I have little time for the 'help me before I watch TV again' crowd, those bored legions intent on indulging their own exasperation. If you want to get all societal about it, the first-order problem is not what Imus and his type say anyway. The problem is that a substantial segment of society enjoys his coarse invective. Or maybe they're just too lazy to turn the channel. I wish someone would get behind inertia as a driving force. How do you refine a coarse society? Now that's a worthy debate. I for one am not sure, though I suspect a coarsened democracy is preferable to a coarsened police state. We inhabit a democracy that tends to stalk equality with a steam-roller's abandon while excellence and merit never speak up for fear of offending someone. Plato, old dead proto-European, suggested that democracy inevitably yields to mediocrity, a fancy way of saying we get exactly what we deserve.

The larger problem is that all major soapboxes in America are controlled by corporations. This is a dismally repetitive dynamic: as corporations sell more soap, they expand into more soapboxes for the express purpose of selling more soap. Solitary voices in the wilderness—the quintessential human voice of poetry for instance—get buried beneath a wall of commercial sound; advertising jingles and their enabling pitchmen—Imus and others—are paid to keep our eyes and ears riveted between commercials. If they ever train soap to tell jokes, that's exactly what we'll get, and judging by this year's Super Bowl ads, the bathwater's making a damn good run at the baby. Rest assured the people tuning into Imus—offended and un-offended alike—were not simultaneously perusing Robert Frost.

Woops, there went an elitist gaffe. But without Oprah's imprimatur, literature just can't peddle soap.

The fact is, the bulk of public speech today, certainly political speech, is underwritten by commercial interests. This is the best argument yet for spending more time listening to your children. Given the alacrity of Imus' demise, the corpocracy's commitment to free speech—despite frequent assertions to the contrary—is almost comically facile even by the lax standards of superficiality. But this is tossing apples in with oranges again. Why should we expect a corporation to revere free speech? Shame on us for thinking that it might. Ostensibly, the public owns the airwaves and licenses those airwaves through the FCC, the People's regulatory designee. Yeah right. If you want to access your fellow citizens on a significant scale, your free speech must bend (stoop?) to the demands of commercial speech. Media corporations take full advantage of the public airwaves by acquiring cost-prohibitive infrastructure, something the average guy's budget precludes. Hey, speech ain't really free. You wanna talk? Tow the party line. Thus funny things happen on the way to the microphone. Serious commentators sprout red noses and big floppy shoes.

The only fail-safe venue for free speech in America today is the one where you can be sure nobody's listening. Think Winston Smith's interior monologue outside the prying apparatus of Big Brother's ubiquitous listening devices. So keep it between yourself and your showerhead Bub—just check the towel rack for wires first.

Alas free speech has no sponsors. Whereas some faction or other will always rise to defend the offended-du-jour, in this instance the Rutgers girls' basketball team. Yes that's right. The offended class is a revolving designation. In Warholian fashion, we will all writhe through our own fifteen minutes of offense. In a properly functioning free society, everyone gets his time on the blocks—call it equality of outrage—though sadly some are the butt of insult more than others. For those sufferers of perennial offense (and let me say for the record I sincerely believe some groups are preyed upon more than others) that is a cultural dysfunction to be addressed through social policy measures, not constitutional disfigurement. In the meantime, the alarming truncation of free speech has the feel of Martin Buber's thorny construct—the problem beneath the problem. Unplugging microphones merely disguises the symptoms of an underlying pathology—racism, xenophobia, religiosity, exceptionalism. It's Freudian repression practiced at a societal level.

The more microphones we have, the uglier we will sound. But if that's who we are, then so be it. The truth might hurt. But self-loathing can be a wonderful motivator. How else can we hope to clean ourselves up?

MR. PRIME MINISTER?

We haven't had to scrutinize our Presidents for despotic intent. In due course we could throw the bum out, or else Congress, jealous of its own Constitutional prerogatives, could take steps to rein in an overzealous executive. However party politics are asserting their affinities across the traditional branches of government with a partisan urgency that, increasingly, dulls the gears of our venerable checks and balances. As a 21st century parliamentarian might counsel an 18th century Jeffersonian, four years can be a long time without some recourse to change.

Indeed one wonders just how egregious executive abuse must become before a Congress, dominated by one party, would contemplate impeaching a President of its own stripe. Lashed together by common ideology, purpose and patronage, what political machine would foreclose on its own bully pulpit? Moreover how could party disunity—on the basis of principle—ever be explained to benefactors who have expended vast sums of money to achieve precisely this end: the securing of two branches of government under one party banner?

Political parties have long been identified as mischief-makers. When a society's constituents identify more keenly with their minority characteristics, the undifferentiated interests of society suffer. Social harmony depends on the recognition of an overarching *commonweal* whose basic welfare precedes the expression of special interests. Why convene a society if this were not the case?

Factions coalesce for the purpose of vaulting their interests above the fray. At the extremes of group formation, no great advantage can be perceived in championing the fray itself. Undue attention to differentiated identities—black, male, rich, gay, Catholic, Anglo-Saxon—can leave America paradoxically unheralded. Thus in times of acute factional rancor, the nation itself goes begging for an earnest spokesman.

Given the current tyranny of party lines, it is refreshing when a national conscience is articulated. A recent example was the late Senator Robert Byrd's speech on the eve of Gulf War II—before an appropriately deserted Senate chamber. Bemoaning the absence of deliberation by his legislative colleagues on a matter as grave as war (even among those within his own opposition party), Byrd was at once achingly quixotic and quintessentially American. A latter-day iconoclast for his insistence on holding deliberation in high esteem, Byrd regarded debate not simply as sound-bite fodder or the obligatory wagging of tongues, but the 'solemn duty' that separates vigorous legislative democracy from ceremonial obsolescence or dictatorial fiat. Like a venerable time capsule, he recorded (prophetically one might suggest) the tragic implications of the abdication:

> "A pall has fallen over the Senate Chamber. We avoid our solemn duty to debate the one topic on the minds of all Americans, even while scores of thousands of our sons and daughters faithfully do their duty in Iraq."

Indeed if not Congress, then who should speak for America's multifarious sons and daughters when common peril threatens? Abject congressional subservience to the Executive mocks the democratic tradition. This is particularly true when the silence is not attributable to genuine unanimity of national purpose, but rather facile party loyalty or tactically-derived opposition party quiescence.

In *Federalist No. 10*, James Madison expresses the hope, naïve perhaps, that the creation of a national Republic would help blunt the more brazen tendencies of parochial interests. Given their general sobriety of purpose, "enlightened statesmen" could be expected to step in and quash localized groundswells of unbridled passion. In his fear of the potentially tyrannous rabble, Madison was clearly displaying more republican than democratic tendencies (lower-case in both instances.) His provincial fixations, like period dress, are best understood in the context of the era, a barely-post-colonial America where prevailing interests were largely indistinguishable from the regions they called home; for example, the manufacturing centers and mercantile interests of the North and the agrarian, landed interests of the South.

Because the states preceded the union as sovereignties, their regional predilections had to be courted. After all, they were being asked to relinquish power to a larger unifying entity, a more-perfect union. To the Founding Fathers' credit, people tend to identify themselves today more as Americans than citizens of a given state. But the decline of regional factionalism hardly ended factionalism. Only the cessation of human nature could do that. Instead, factions have sprouted along less regionally-beholden themes e.g. social/moral tastes (abortion, capital punishment), demography (social security, Medicare) and guild (lawyers, HMO providers, etc.)

Resorting to rhetorical irony, Madison suggested the only sure way to kill factionalism was to "destroy the liberty which is essential to its existence;" a cure, he realized, immeasurably worse than the disease. What Madison seems not to have envisioned was a system where his enlightened statesmen, those unclouded by "factious tempers, local prejudices or sinister designs" might be driven from power altogether. Not by roving bands of pitchfork-wielding peasantry, but by well-financed, organizationally astute factions, i.e. modern political parties and their well-heeled benefactors.

To be fair, Madison could never have imagined modern American corporatism with its huge concentrations of wealth and the mischief such wealth wreaks through the financing of political campaigns. A survey-history of American political parties exceeds the scope of this essay. Suffice to say that, as the republic grew both in geographic and economic scale, powerful interests, ever more powerful themselves, went to greater lengths to retain their advantages.

As the reservoir of power expanded, more lay at stake with every contemplated power-exchange.

Madison sought to blunt factionalism in a larger republic. On this point at least, Montesquieu may have proven the more adroit of the two as, thirty years earlier, he had argued: "It is in the nature of a republic that it has only a small territory: without that it could scarcely exist."

Grappling with size in a distinctly geographic context, Daniel Boorstin points to its salutary effects throughout America's development. In his collection of essays, *Hidden History*, he describes the *tonic of distance*—how the sheer immensity of America was itself a salve to factional mischief. The country's vastness simply swallowed various sects and group eccentricities before sectarian discord could take root. If one town disparaged a certain congregational practice, the minority practitioners could start a new town somewhere else. The place was so in need of being filled up, sectarian battles were rare. Nonetheless the common thread in these men's thinking was that the scale of the enterprise played a role in democracy's operation.

Madison or his contemporaries could not possibly have foreseen modern parliamentary government. At least in a parliamentary system, the functional head, the prime minister, can fall to a no-confidence vote within his own party, or call for new elections to re-affirm his party's mandate. Short of the rather draconian—and institutionally perilous—impeachment process, no such mechanism of expulsion exists in the American system beyond the four-year presidential election cycle.

In its recent drift to more overt expressions of party politics, America may be emulating, in some respects, the parliamentary model. In 1787, Europe was still grappling with monarchies and had only begun to evolve a workable system. But as Robert Dahl points out in *How Democratic Is the American Constitution*, America, suddenly the venerable old lady, is the only country—among the twenty-two advanced democracies—claiming a bona fide presidential system. The rest are, to varying degrees, parliamentary democracies. Thus Madison's necessary evils now form the pillars of government in modern democracies.

Could it be America is imitating the least attractive parliamentary practices while retaining the worst presidential themes? Today's Congress is awash in men and women of 'factious temper'—Madison's pejorative term for party loyalists. Tom DeLay built a congressional dynasty on the 'strength' of factious temper. He reveled in his nickname, The Hammer, a tool renowned for its blunt force, hardly emblematic of Jeffersonian temperance.

The age-old vices of greed and power-lust excel at recruiting men and women to their many causes while ostracizing those who defy them when principled opposition compels. This culling process works to excise civic virtue from government. The powers-that-be, no great Constitutional sentimentalists, have created a meritocracy-in-reverse which, if Plato can be believed, suggests the very definition of a mediocracy.

We can be assured the abandonment of constitutional exactitude for party loyalty does not spring from a renewed commitment to national interests, even when the national moment cries out for transcending leaders. If the essence of statesmanship is the suspension of narrow self-interest for the purpose of championing a larger cause, then who, among our elected partisans, will be the champions? And if not the current crop of incumbents, what magnitude of calamity will coax the best and brightest back into the public arena? One shudders to think.

While mediocrities might make the best functionaries, the party's interests often come at the Republic's peril. During times when strange new crises appear, a sort of veering pragmatism, FDR's 'trying everything until something works' can be the best leadership credo. However this non-programmatic style has the potential to color outside the lines of factional interests. If anything, parties demand a sort of dull predictability from their anointed—the better to raise money from their perennial, identifiable interests.

Democracy allows no panacea. In the end, we must judge between the lesser of two evils. That said, perhaps the only thing worse than a fractious two-party system is a de facto one-party system.

Our current President, no stranger to absolutist tendencies, has been emboldened by his party's dominance across all three branches of government (the Supreme Court can be included), weathering only the most facile objections from his partisans not to mention embarrassing silence from a cowed Democratic opposition. An uncontested mind, barricaded by absolute power, can spawn strange notions. It's not surprising then that, lacking an oppositional force, Bush has blazed an extra-constitutional trail of a distinct authoritarian bent. The rationale, we are told, for unauthorized wire-taps, overseas gulags, warrant-less searches and the like is that a liberal democracy must confront Islamo-fascism with fascism countermeasures of its own. Later, at some indeterminate point (presumably when the war on terror, notorious for its amorphous objectives, has been fully prosecuted and the enemy's scalp is on the mantel piece), Madison's beloved republic can be resumed.

That is, if we haven't become our own worst enemy first. Ben Franklin, for one, would have few good things to say of a nation that jettisons hard-won liberty in a bid for hermetic security. Long before the Great American Experiment, Odysseus discovered the real battle often begins with the journey home. The Gulf War II ticker-tape parade, commenced on the deck of an aircraft carrier, is now nearly two years old. Still we wait for Godot. Meanwhile the interminable mission (whatever it is no reasonable person can say) rolls along, answerable it seems only to itself.

One might ask, why assemble an evil axis if the purpose isn't to rehabilitate the entire membership? In the true Orwellian sense of perma-war, this conflict has the complexion of a generational undertaking. Surely one formidable American faction, the military industrial complex, rejoices over such an existential, and self-manufacturing adversary as abject terror. There isn't a missile in the world that can vanquish terror. However there is always a defense contractor willing to pursue the R&D for it. Once upon a time in a war long ago, we had nothing to fear but fear itself. Today we wage a war against fear. What would FDR say?

But what if, despite our current President's best ministrations, Armageddon doesn't come? What if, after defeating Islamo-fascism, we never make it back to who we were, and get stuck being something else entirely? There are many things worse than the fractious divisiveness of democracy, the monolith of Big Brotherhood for one.

Heraclitus, pre-Socratic philosopher and early opponent of George Bush's static universe, wrote of enantiadromia: anything, driven to its extreme, eventually runs out of itself, becoming its polar opposite. Orwell captured enantiadromia-in-language with his famous slogans from *1984*, *love is hate, war is peace*. Language on the cusp of embracing its opposition is the harbinger of a world at the tipping point. We inhabit a moment in history, it seems, when time-worn homilies are being turned on their heads. Are we coming to embrace everything we have traditionally abhorred?

Our current President perceives the world as a series of fixed battlements. *Our* good struggles, with implacable resoluteness, against *their* evil. This almost-hysterical self-righteousness is a clarion call for an imminent enantiadromic reversal. George Bush, spokesman for such Orwellian bromides as *peace through war*, offers the same lifeless rhetoric even as the war shifts beneath his feet like a subterranean river. He is at a perpetual loss for revised objectives, seemingly unable to make mid-stream corrections. Only with his looming lame duck status are members of the President's own party finally giving voice to the neglected business of the Republic. Perhaps we should be thankful for the intemperance of ambitious men.

Deprive factions of air, Madison argued, and you risk extinguishing them—and the fire of liberty—forever. Indeed it's rare for a country, once embarked down a totalitarian path, to 're-liberalize' without powerful inducements. Far more common are societies that, tiring of democracy's manifold frustrations, yield to the temptation of a Strong Man. Totalitarianism creeps with cunning efficiency because it enjoys early broad-based support. As for dictators, they start with the best of intentions. The people, often harried, simply want efficiency, security and reliable train schedules. No leader sets out to do irreparable harm to his country. Indeed authoritarians are always the last to see their own ebbing benevolence. Romania's Ceausescu was arrogant and intransigent until his back was literally to the wall—where he was summarily machine-gunned to death.

At this moment in history, we should understand that our President in many respects aspires to the role of Maximum Prime Minister. Buoyed by a listless opposition on one side, dutiful apparatchiks on the other, and Constitutional legitimacy until 2008, he—and us—suffer for lack of a spirited opposition. Yes, his cause may once have been just, if abysmally executed. But in America, ends have never been allowed to justify means. Instead we hold ourselves to a higher bar: the manner in which justice is achieved must itself conform to just conduct. The Constitution protects us from overreaching zealots, no matter how well-intentioned. Now if we can only find someone to man its levers.

BACK TO THE FUTURE WITH GUERNICA: THE SENTIMENTAL IMPULSE AND THE FUNDAMENTALIST APPEAL

"My whole life as an artist has been nothing more than a continuous struggle against reaction and the death of art."—Picasso, on Guernica

Picasso was asked repeatedly to explain the meaning behind his paintings as though the paintings themselves were perfunctory blueprints to be rifled for their precious contents. But why attempt a canvas when an arcane treatise will do? Picasso addressed this question often, pouring varying degrees of scorn on those with the temerity to ask for assistive viewing devices. Who could blame him? When people queried him for what he *really* meant, were they not asking him in effect to abandon the act of painting and become a tour-guide instead? Robert Frost's famous retort comes to mind when he too was asked to deconstruct his art into talking points: "Would you have me say it in more or less-adequate words?" Art is not a straw man. Helpful to us in our daily lives—for example as a way-station for interpretive reflection—it has its own reality to uphold. Moreover the artist's recourse to imagery is a pre-reflective phenomenon, not an explicit stratagem. The latter would suggest more propaganda than art.

This is not to say *Guernica* doesn't offer a political dimension laden with symbols. Indeed the political context of the piece serves only to amplify the popular clamor for bite-sized meaning. Subservient minds, when they petition the artist for interpretive cues, are really seeking the apt permissioning. Their own discerning powers too atrophied, perhaps too cowed, to attempt an unassisted apprehension of the art, they want to be told what is meant by the bull, the horse, the light, the arm, the baby—beyond of course what their eyes tell them they see—a bull, a horse, a light, an arm and a baby.

But irony of ironies, an artist's interrogation by an audience eager for instruction is precisely the soil within which fascism takes hold. Tell us what to feel, oh Aesthetic Leader. Thus Picasso, in fulfilling his prophetic obligations, encountered the unthinkingness that Hannah Arendt identifies in her 1952 landmark book *The Origins of Totalitarianism* as the essential ingredient of all totalitarian societies. This is a circuitous way of saying Picasso's warnings fell on ears already deaf to prophetic remonstrance. There is a tragicomic element here as the mineshaft canary, the artist, expires magnificently only to be trampled beneath the feet of oblivious miners.

The tragic irony weaves ever deeper as Guernica graphically outlines the 'honest terror' of the modern age (Lorca's term) driving people into two wrong-directed and unthinkingly reactive modes 1) (backwards) flights to the past and 2) (heavenwards) petitioning a godless sky. Of course these retro-modes represent futurist visions in the most superficial sense as they claim the future for the purpose only of resurrecting an idealized past.

Thus one of the more striking aspects of *Guernica* is the utter absence of progress. The future is in full recoil from itself. Nothing is moving forward. No one, not man, woman or beast is even facing forward. When the present moment is compelled to mimic a past that can never be revisited, it becomes an inauthentic present, a toxic nostalgia. Picasso's *Guernica* figures are displaying, either in their heavenward beseeching of an absented god or in their attempt to light a path back to the future (the Enlightenment in retreat), a desire to, in Arendt's words "…escape from the grimness of the present into nostalgia for a still intact past, or into the anticipated oblivion of a better future."

This amnesia project is as immense as it is hopelessly escapist. The petitioning of an answerable god, particularly in its more fundamentalist permutations, must first strive to forget the indelible legacies of such giants as Nietzsche and Heidegger, just as a time-battered creationism must ignore the practically unassailable: Darwinism, the fossil record, the DNA, Dawkin's selfish gene and modern physic's fourteen-billion-light-year-old universe. The past is lost except in weird parody. The only valid strategy is to exist authentically in the present, no matter how terrifying that present may be. One wonders what Picasso was intuiting in our future that such a wholesale retreat from it is warranted. Auschwitz would follow, as would the killing fields of Cambodia as would the ethnic cleansing of Yugoslavia as would the tribal genocide in Rwanda. One shudders to think these could be mere preludes to something more terrible still.

We can blame Nazi Germany for unleashing a war of symbols in Guernica. As Russell Martin suggests in his book *Picasso's War*, the Luftwaffe's attack on the town represented "the first time in modern warfare that a target had been destroyed solely for symbolic reasons." So Picasso is merely moving the metaphors forward. In fact his explicit symbols symbolize the flagging symbols of culture. That's right. The symbols are, in one sense, symbolic of symbological disarray, that is, cultural inarticulateness. Our cultural predilections long since exposed as serviceable affectations in the face of brutal onslaught—mere flotsam and jetsam, a bull here and a sword there—all of it appears as being washed downstream in a powerful current of nihilistic oblivion. In a recent essay (*A New Literacy, The Kenyon Review, 24:1, Winter 2007, 10-24*) George Steiner noted the utter failure of culture to avert the Holocaust, indeed to find an existence alongside it:

> "Twentieth-century barbarism sprang from within the heartland of Europe culture, from the very center of the philosophic, aesthetic, and classical education. The death camps were not built in the Gobi Desert. And when barbarism challenged, the humanities, the arts, philosophic thought proved not only largely impotent but often collaborative with despotism and

massacre. The actual designation *literae humaniores* rang hollow."

Picasso in *Guernica* is depicting the holocaust that corrodes culture under the twin-assault of totalitarianism and religious fundamentalism. Would it surprise Picasso that the early years of the 21st century have been dominated by the reactionary wings of the resurgent, millennia-old Abrahamic faiths? *Guernica* tells us the future lies in a deep yearning for the past. What awaits us? Only time will tell.

WHY A WHITE MAN SHOUTING 'RACE!' ALWAYS MAKES A SHRILL SOUND IN A CROWDED THEATRE

I will now be assuming my quintessential role as a middle-aged white man, a role which typecasts me without mercy. It remains to be seen what color I've taken in the reader's mind by the end. Probably the best that can be hoped for is an off-off-white. To be without color is to be an apparition—not of this world.

So my skin lies draped across the dais like a pale effigy. Revealing the hue behind the words, I suspect, wins me a slew of deaf ears, the ones that listen from the inside-out, cued to the stereotypes that govern most minds. But we shouldn't be too hard on ourselves. A mind is a reductionist machine lashed to a shotgun blast of random data points. We reduce to live.

Perhaps this rather sensible survival skill redounds, inappropriately, into our relations with people. I touch a flame once and burn my finger. Thereafter I regard all future flames with stereotypical disdain. Wisely, I adopt a discriminatory practice towards fire. The danger comes when this mainstay of the scientific method, reductionism, shadows my transactions with people who are neither objects nor disembodied phenomena. Though I might register a bad experience with a person of another group or tribe, if I am to honor the sacred content of individual souls, the extrapolative urge must be resisted. Humanity in the aggregate is an abstraction, becoming meaningful only at the human level. Every human being deserves the dignity of being met—and valued—on his or her own merits. Relegating an individual to a prescribed set of group behaviors or tendencies is, frankly, a de-humanizing tactic.

Noted psychiatrist and Holocaust survivor Victor Frankl put his finger on the darker side of reductionism when he said:

> "it is an approach and procedure that deprives the human phenomena of their very humanness by reducing a human phenomenon in dynamic terms to some sub-human phenomenon, or deducing human phenomena, in genetic terms, from sub-human phenomena."

Groups do not display human behaviors; people do. At best, stereotyping is a form of shorthand or social laziness. At worst, it aids and abets pure evil such as eugenics and 'racial purity' projects.

Unfortunately centuries of stereotyping and jaw-dropping ignorance have left behind a monumental clean-up effort for which furtive dialogue can serve as the initial broom and shovel. And yet, despite the compulsion to talk about race, race resists being talked about. As with many things that form the core of our identities, there is a lingering sense we can never win the full empathy of others. Add to this the horrific legacy of inter-racial strife, and you're left with a bone-dry tinderbox that often tempts the best rhetorical matches. In this way, inter-racial dialogue has become the greased-pole of American discourse. Perhaps we're drawn to articulate the inarticulable with a sort of masochistic resolve. Certainly it blows up in our faces more often than not.

There is always that tantalizing brass ring: full-bodied rapprochement. Such a compelling target can coax the bravest souls out from behind Ellison's invisibility gig in a bid for honest daylight; though the quest may ultimately be quixotic. Each of us has an obligation to try in our own way. For me the temptation takes on a distinctly vocational complexion: Can I write my white away?

The great chasms of the racial divide have swallowed many intrepid explorers. Invariably the templates of ingrained belief rattle against our best efforts to be heard. Race is its own brand of solipsism. Packaged in urban legends, awash in myths, girded by misperceptions, it is also the ultimate subjectivist gambit. I emit an *a priori* groan, knowing I'm about to sound like 'how most white guys sound', a sound as mythic as the white unicorn, but because I am now on record as being white, one that reinforces the dubious mythos with tautological certitude. How self-reinforcing this stereotype business is. At times I think the whole race debate borders on madness. Like an oasis-mirage to the thirsty man, it means everything. Yet there is nothing to it.

One of the great ancillary myths of race is that we possess a perfect understanding of the same-race stranger who sleeps beside us every night. In fact everyone is a stranger to everyone else. Racial unity is a rhetorical exaggeration aimed at making an inter-racial point.

And yet race—both its cohesiveness and its separateness—has evolved to the mythic stature of Big Foot. My race is an indelible footprint that appears even before I put my foot down. I'd fire it as my agent except it's gotten too far beneath the skin of others.

Like many, I have a dream—of striding into a room with a swagger born of un-self-consciousness, overwhelming all crass bids to judge me on the basis of color. But race is affixed to our skin. It follows us everywhere. In a strange sense, my skin becomes the enemy of my identity. I'd shed its delimiting tendencies if I could. Then again, the fantasy of *racelessness* may be a perpetual striving-towards that never offers up a terminus. Or have I underestimated the perniciousness of my quarry; has whiteness penetrated my soul?

There is an asynchronous quality to race. My particular color, compounded frankly by my gender, attracts a mountain of suspicion whenever I show the temerity to expound on race. If I read the enemy correctly, the thinking is 'why would he parade his embarrassment of riches?' Though I am the routine butt of them, I cannot reciprocate with racial jokes of my own. Referencing race casts wary eyes upon me as though I may be trying to retake the plantation. My comments are sifted for prejudicial detritus and the artifactual legacy of Jim Crow.

Up until now, you know very little about me. In all this race-fixation, I have short-shrifted myself. Suffice to say I harbor far too much ambition to become the stalking horse for mere whiteness. I want to gaze down on entire cities with equanimity. A universal blurring of the tribes, I believe, is our only salvation. To the stilted go no spoils.

As to whether whiteness, a biological dearth of melanin, prevailed in establishing a 'hierarchy of pigment' which in turn precipitated reactive sub-cultures, who am I to say? I will only note that if, in our studious efforts to avoid one another, impenetrable sub-cultures formed as a bulwark against the withholding of a larger acceptance, then that is a profound failing of the great American melting pot. Verily, we will rue the separation.

The larger more sociological implications notwithstanding, I cling to the belief that, when I open my mouth, something more than whiteness spills forth. Perhaps a little humanity, glints of an untinted soul. Moreover I chafe at being reduced to what I deem to be the false-totality of my whiteness. For one thing, it's rather racist. A conscientious objector, I reserve part of myself for something other than race.

Before I acquiesced to freckles, I possessed an unblemished soul. God told me this in so many words that at times possessed the motive force of sticks and stones. Are wounds allowed? My scars are more red than white. You might say my pigment's engrossed in a sex-change of sorts. Please excuse me as my voice goes through a series of inalterable changes. But before I'm done here, I want to be hard to peg, scarred to a blank, dead lifelessness that lurks beyond all reasonable attempts to assess my prior, living color. If I died trying not to be white, would you forgive me the plantation whips that, ironically, neither I nor my direct forbears ever wielded?

Though quite a mouthful, race is less a word than it is a sordid past trying desperately to erase itself into a better future. My color puts me on the wrong side of the historic equation. But what's an equation between incalculable souls? Erase my whiteness and—it is my hope—you'd be left with the inky blankness of soul-content. And yes, though I am not a wealthy man, I have no doubt been assisted in hundreds of unseen ways. I am a believer in the unseen. Recently on National Public Radio an African-American listener called in citing Hillary Clinton's invocation of "hard-working white blue-collar Americans". His point was that the deployment of 'hard-working' as an adjective for 'white' was patently racist. This was an epiphany for me. He was right of course. But I had not heard the racial slur (just as I'm sure Clinton, eager to woo the black vote, could not have intended it.) How many other racist codes I wondered are stored in our vocabularies beyond our fields of apprehension?

The fact is whiteness has become a near-synonym for privilege, expropriation and exploitation, stacking more chips in my corner than I can recognize, let alone count. That I am male—a further boon—dooms me with paradoxical insistency even further still. Being on top of the pecking order has been no picnic, my swarthy complexioned, ever-wary and sometimes female friends! As the white male monolith falls into abeyance, you will have your chance. Though why you persist in your envy is a source of bewilderment to me. I'm convinced resentment always has an envious component.

At its histrionic apogee, race-gender 'logic' seems to question, almost laughably, 'how on God's tactfully green earth a white man can suffer adversity.' Never mind that attempting to inoculate white men from the more sordid afflictions of the world seems almost to anoint them with the mastery that at times they have been accused of seeking for themselves. Perhaps you haven't been looking of late. We're far from scary, and hardly the Nietzschean supermen of contra-racial lore. Time does not allow me to catalog the tribulations of white men. First I'd need to ponder the reality of a peculiarly derived white man's burden. My sense is this is an historic fiction, spun entirely from whole white cloth.

Who's kidding whom? A cross-check of lists between races would offer much the same catalog of ills. The operative term is a common humanity. It may bear little relevance to the contexts in which other groups elect to engage us, but when a white guy goes home, properly demystified, he hugs his children tenderly, maybe writhes in agony with a bad back or pains over the loss of a loved one. The truth is, when observed outside the narrow context of the subjugation model, some of us can be eminently nice fellows.

Modern DNA and genealogical study unequivocally points to the crucial similarities of human beings. The differences are *de minimus*. We should thank God that modern science is proving an ally in the de-escalation of race consciousness. There'd be a heap more trouble if race actually carried some empirical gravitas. For the record, I've met too many exceptional people from other races—and too many dunderheads from my own—to ever have seriously entertained a racial-mastery-complex. Nonetheless good hard science is a welcome further blow to this insidious conceit.

As for my race, I find it regarded much like carbon monoxide: tasteless, colorless and altogether rather bland. Largely a province of historic privilege, it bears little inspection beyond its predatory zeal. Outside some flaky, white supremacist circles, there is little conscious pride that derives from being white. Or is my own diminished self-esteem showing here? Then there's the horrendously begged question: 'white *what*'? Lithuanian, Scottish, Norwegian? It seems there are myriad languages and cultures sloshing about beneath the white umbrella, really more skeletal hub-and-spoke than defining canopy.

Here's the test, Dr. Skinner: a white American finds himself on a deserted island with two fellow male companions, a Swede and an African-American. Let's keep them all straight to avoid sexual politics. Whom would the white American naturally gravitate towards for camaraderie? The guy who could talk NCAA basketball and American politics or the guy, similarly complexioned, who speaks only Swedish and has a passion for hockey? My hypothetical island is a tropical one, thus making hockey even less engaging banter over a splash of Crusoe's best coconut juice. Perhaps I've offended my Swedish readers with an unconscionable stereotype. You're all avid hockey players, yes?

There are few contexts in which a white guy can deploy the term 'race' without incurring the wrath of someone on the 'other side'. We all have beefs. I am aware of exasperation among many white people that practically no dialogue of a defining criticality is allowed them on the subject of race. When they do offer an observation, proper etiquette demands a contritional tone; all statements must be prefaced with an acknowledgement of guilt and past sins like a lame PSA. In fairness, these protestations carry some merit. Of course there is the ultimate show-stopper 'I was born one-hundred years after the abolition of slavery', and the more passive aggressive rejoinder, 'My grandfather was Irish-American and couldn't get a job either.' Many whites came to America as indentured servants. The African slave trade relied on the complicity of many black Africans. I happen to be Scottish. Forcibly displaced from their homeland, many of my countrymen arrived on cramped cattle boats that didn't even enjoy the regulatory oversight afforded African slave ships. There, have we shifted enough bases?

Frankly this is all a pointless 'my dad's tougher than your dad' contest. Suffering is a universal phenomenon that happens at the personal level. Groups are abstractions. People feel pain. Some individuals are destined to suffer more than others. Must we stack the suffering into racial piles to see whose catalog of misery reaches the sun first? To what end? I say, far better to channel our energies towards present-day suffering with a zeal attended by ardent color-blindness. Is there merit to African-American reparation movements? I'm not qualified to say. But yes, I see the bones of an argument even as I see an avalanche of like-minded claims from other aggrieved social groups. We nurse wounds of varied complexion.

I can't say Reverend Al Sharpton is a demagogue. I have to *wait* for a black person to render that judgment. Only then might I be allowed to echo the sentiment, but in a circumspect, reserved manner. I must censor myself in deference to racial sensitivities, no matter the veracity of my opinion. Thus I can never vilify a black public personage with passionate glee. I love passionate glee. All my best vitriol must be reserved from white guys. Fortunately, there's no shortage of white dudes to vilify.

Is self-loathing allowed in a war of pigmentation? There is the vaguest hint of a patronizing tone afoot in this essay. I sense it as I hold forth, instructing on whiteness. But what else can I do? How can it be expunged? Or does retribution involve being skinned alive? I'm rather comfortable in my skin that is I hardly notice it until I encounter the skin of others. It's only then that I become aware of having a skin at all.

I believe we are still a long way off from being judged solely by the content of our characters—even as I also believe we've come a very long way indeed. Barack Obama may be a shining example of our progress. Or is he? The guy's a walking Rorschach test. We all intersect in him. But are we merely bathing in our own reflection or savoring the contiguous reflections of others?

In a recent *Prospect* essay, (*"Healing Postponed";* March 2008), social commentator—and I feel obliged to add, Black Briton—Trevor Phillips suggests that Obama's promise of racial healing is nothing more than a cynical ploy offered up by a savvy politician. Echoing themes from Shelby Steele's book *A Bound Man: Why We Are Excited About Obama and Why He Can't Win*, Phillips suggests that Obama belongs to that school of upwardly mobile African-Americans known as 'bargainers'. This genus pursues a different tack than the 'challengers', those 'uppity' types who, like Malcolm X and Marcus Garvey, seek to make no great ally of the white majority. The bargainers by comparison, "strike quite a different deal by saying to white America: "I will not use America's horrible history of white racism against you, if you will promise not to use my race against me." That way, everybody wins; whites feel flattered and win back what Steele calls their "racial innocence." Blacks acquire freedom from the cage of their colour (sic)."

In the end, Phillips concludes with Steele that this bargain is more Faustian than anything else; answerable to personal ambition in the first instance and perhaps even injurious to a broader progressive agenda. And because both challengers and bargainers prosper from racism, each needs "the racial divide to stay at the centre of US life. In truth, Obama may be helping to postpone the arrival of a post-racial America…" How the Gordian knot of racial politics never disappoints.

A mere writer, I have smaller fish to fry. However should my character prove to be inalterably white, as is suggested in some quarters, then forgive the glorious false trail of this essay. Perhaps my bid for depth is undone by an unyielding surface tension. But racial unawareness is an enviable ideal worthy of tireless pursuit. Though it may never be attained, we should endeavor towards a Great Forgetting with every skin cell of our being.

By now I've probably registered an overdraft in my historical allowance. For my part, I choose to notch an awareness of where we are in the grand racial reconciliation, concede its present state of incompletion, and censor my tongue accordingly. I believe in judicious self-censorship if it furthers the commonweal—call it the little white lies of omission. After all my tongue is not an island (as I find many white people endeavoring to believe), but an appendage linked to a past I didn't inhabit, but yet strangely embody, and in some sense bear a responsibility for. Forbearance is the least I can offer on this, our delicate, perilous road to racial rapprochement. May we one day see one another, soul-to-soul, on the other side.

IN A GLOBAL VILLAGE, NO ONE CAN HEAR YOU SCREAM

Television broadcasting in the U. S. has been dying a protracted death for many years, it's just that nobody bothered to notice. The parent networks NBC, ABC, CBS and FOX will surely survive, albeit in significantly diminished form. But the many small affiliate stations that dot the country, some no more than mom and pop concerns, face uncertain futures. No longer gilded fortresses with licenses to print money, over-the-air broadcasters face increasing competition from many sources, most notably cable and direct broadcast satellite (DBS), like Rupert Murdoch's DirecTV. Quite simply, the affiliates have failed, over twenty years, to carve out a 'post-broadcast' identity for themselves. Instead they have assented to being carried on non-broadcast cable and DBS feeds, inviting a sort of self-imposed euthanasia.

With the meteoric rise of cable and satellite television, it is conceivable that the Tiffany Network and the Glorious Peacock could one day command all the cache—and viewership—of Food TV. But only if Brian Williams can whip up a good soufflé. And in case anyone hasn't noticed, Comcast, the largest cable system (and the largest content buyer) has been flexing its purchasing power of late, negotiating bruising deals with its providers. Content may be what draws the eyeballs to the TV screen, but the pipe still wears the pants.

During its formative years, cable relied heavily on broadcast network programming. Appropriately, the industry's focus was on building out its cable infrastructure. Television content origination was a luxury reserved for the cash-rich broadcasters. For a cable system, the local network affiliate was the equivalent of the anchor store at a mall. It provided a critical mass around which lesser venues could cluster. In time, those 'lesser venues' (Discovery, Animal Planet, The History Channel, HBO, etc.) grew up to command brand name stature in their own right. The original consumer selling point was not cable programming, but improved reception of over-the-air stations via coaxial cable. Believe it or not, many people actually liked their programming, and were willing to pay a few bucks to get a better picture via cable.

But now the training wheels are off and it's the cable guy holding the remote. Cable networks are making the networks prove their value—what a rude departure from the days when cable begged permission to carry the local affiliates. Indeed what a horrible strategic blunder on the part of the networks, empowering their competitor's right into the driver's seat. While cable started life as a redundant delivery system, today it's the broadcasters who face possible death-by-redundancy.

A mere ten percent of today's TV watchers take their programming directly from a broadcasting source (as opposed to 80% in 1985). Most receive their 'over-the-air' network content via cable (80 per cent) or DBS (10 per cent). This represents a staggering decline, not to mention a perilous end-run, for the broadcasters. Even though most viewers have abandoned free broadcast TV for pay alternatives, simply having the free TV option lends some pricing discipline to cable and satellite providers. Without broadcast TV, pay TV subscription rates will certainly continue their upward trend, and at a re-doubled pace.

Aside from their role in controlling cable prices, why would anyone care about the poor affiliate stations? Well, they're the last leg of the media landscape with any 'community service' impulse left. Affiliate stations' local TV news programs are still most Americans' go-to source for regional news and events. Radio consolidation succeeded in killing community radio and enshrining Howard Stern. Newspapers' circulation numbers are on a fast sprint to oblivion. Think public access television is the ultimate solution? Ask anyone at your local cable company's public access channel what Viacom and Cox think of their 'public duty' to carry those tacky little citizen shows. They hate it and would love nothing more than to commandeer the channel for Home Improvement: The Basement Network. Despite the fair criticisms that can be lodged against local TV news shows, they provide a source of local information. Call me paranoid, but it almost seems like someone doesn't want us to know what's going on in our own neighborhoods.

To echo Tip O'Neill, all news is local. For instance, the tragedy of war becomes suddenly more authentic when we learn about the young guy in the neighboring town getting killed. Hey, he went to the same mall we did. By contrast, the faceless casualty numbers that flash across national media outlets have an obligatory, disembodied quality. I believe we're talking here about the abstract nature of statistics, damned statistics, versus bringing it on home. Local news excels at putting a face on the larger event. Whereas globalism prefers to traffic in the faceless masses—the less empathy they can evoke within us, the more alienated we feel. This is good for business.

When the big guys think about local-based programs they get return-on-investment indigestion; just think of all those duplicative production costs. Bean-counters to the bone, they want to shove one program down the pipe. Why create numerous versions of crap when you can get away with one big monolithic piece of crap? And don't give me all that global village hooey. Like most Americans, my stomping grounds still consist of a 30-square mile patch—and I want to know something about it.

There is still some hope for the affiliates—if they can show some strategic gumption. The future, should they seek to have one, lies in multicasting. Using the digital broadcast spectrum each current station has been assigned as part of a high-definition television (HDTV) transition, a cluster of digital broadcast channels could be offered regionally, in effect creating a localized 'mini-cable' system in crisp, clear digital format.

The parent networks oppose multicasting and plan to feed the affiliates with a single HDTV signal, so the affiliates would be on their own to create this sort of service. But if they don't take advantage of the one real benefit they provide to viewers—localism—local TV stations will soon become one casualty in a long line of community-focused resources. It's up to the local broadcasters, and the local media advocates, to ensure that a significant space for localism is carved out in the brave new digital world.

NOTHING BUT NIHILISM

"There may actually be puritanical fanatics of conscience who prefer even a certain nothing to an uncertain something to lie down on—and die. But this is nihilism and the sign of a despairing, mortally weary soul..."—Frederick Nietzsche, *Beyond Good and Evil*

These days there's a whole lot of nothing going on, and its exploits are the subject of keen reportage. The eschatological branches of Christianity, Islam and Judaism are all abuzz at the imminent fruition of their grim projects. Even the great secular stories are looking a bit long in the tooth. For example, no one expects to get bailed out by an advancing enlightenment or scientific progress anymore. Marxism went belly-up. Liberalism is wilting in the face of resurgent fascist tendencies. With everything ending at once, it's hard to know where to begin.

Nihilists are the most traumatized orphans of the world's many collapsing stories. Dispirited idealists, they yearn for something to lie down on; a creed, a hammock, a coffin, it hardly matters. The extreme branches of organized religion offer just what the mortally weary ordered: a morally-sanctioned end-game. What's less clear is the media's elected role as willing matchmaker to this nihilistic despair, inviting aggrieved parties everywhere to cobble their resentments.

With twenty-four hours to kill and a penchant for big bangs, television is the great enabler. Once, scruffy malcontents dotted every province. Now they draw strength from milling, televised crowds. Suddenly the world faces global affiliations of ideological warriors locked in titanic struggles. For anyone doubting the incendiary power of language, the resultant conflagrations are captured daily on videotape.

I'm reminded of a certain intrepid newscaster tethered to a pole in Florida during the very early stages of a pre-Katrina hurricane. As he tried mightily to talk the storm up, his body bent at a dramatic 25-degree angle, an old man shuffled across the foreground unimpaired. There isn't a reporter chasing an ambulance who doesn't dream of doing something really important. He wants to chronicle a *movement*. Those journalists blessed with proximity to the carnage seize their career-making moments with relish. The current bumper crop of dispirited souls provides a ready source of combustible material with the blood of innocents merely heightening the dramatic arc. Whether they realize it or not, journalists are in the business, not of fact gathering, but of manufacturing narrative, which in turn incites further violence.

Is the chattering class oblivious to the perils of mindless chatter? Perhaps they should teach more modern philosophy in journalism school. Far from being Plato's chaste-bearers-of-ideas, language is like the girl who lives on the hill: loose and endlessly accommodating. Wittgenstein blasted the metaphysician's tendency to flatter language as a 'pure intermediary.' Why else would 'family values' tumble from the mouths of Dr. James Dobson and Howard Dean with seeming profound singularity? People only think they've delineated their friends and beliefs with metaphysical certitude. In fact, their words court many darlings. It pays to do a background check on your own cherished rhetoric.

Perhaps the Surgeon General should affix warning labels to dictionaries, or at least to Bibles, Q'rans and Torahs. Toss about a few ill-chosen words and monotheisms can turn monomaniacal in a flash. That's why nihilism travels so well under religious cover. You say Yahweh, I say Tomah-to and a fight breaks out. Once a name gives birth to a god (and allowing for a reasonable period to establish a dogma and hire some clergy), the newly minted Universal sets out to undermine all competing Universals. Crusades, jihads, pogroms, inquisitions, holocausts, fatwahs, dust-ups; pick the language of your poison. Hey gang, there may be many paths up the mountain, but if you catch anyone using an alternate path, you have my permission to kick their ass. Now go be fruitful and multiply.

This essay is not an attempt to press a nihilistic agenda on the very existence of God. There are sharp distinctions between the gods of organized traditions and what Jung described as a personal experience with the numinous, his definition of an 'authentic' religious experience. Unfortunately, the latter has proven itself stubbornly resistant to transpersonal conveyance as the devil always lays waiting in the dogma. By all rights, contemplative silence should command a larger audience. But as it refuses to speak up for itself, few demagogues rise to its occasion.

Like Jung, Kierkegaard balked at the cumulus-robed-God-with-sandals, arguing for an essentially interior deity, a manifestation of 'sheer personality'. He devoted entire books to the gulf that separated the Christian god of organized religion from the Christian god of inner experience. To put it mildly, the bearded-guy-in-the-clouds folks bristle at the notion of God as a 'mere' psychologic reality (the psyche, as Jung would say, is everything, and thus no small thing.) People are quite fond of their anthropomorphic apparitions, thank you very much.

Take away God's arms and legs and you're left with a sublime blob of narrative inertia. Indeed religion, the organized kind, would not travel far without language, its propagator. History seems to plod along uneventfully enough until God discards a match, sending a bush into theophanic flames. In those precious careless moments, some human intermediary catches an earful, transcribing it onto the nearest available medium. That same instant, those outside the prophet's sphere of influence acquire a whole new cadre of sworn enemies. Nietzsche was unequivocal: "If a temple is to be erected *a temple must be destroyed*" (his italics). Not surprisingly, the trouble starts in the literalist camps where a god's choice of language becomes the focus of idolatrous fixation. Holding God to every inflection has proved a lethal business. How many times has "an eye for an eye" been trundled out for the sole purpose of zapping some mentally-incapacitated black guy in Texas?

Years ago, I heard a very wise rabbi politely debunk comparative religious studies as 'trans-empirical fallacies'. Though the implications are grim for inter-faith relations, he was on to an excellent point. Attempts to spark authentic, sustained dialogue across monotheistic traditions are akin to rubbing two novels against one another in the hope they launch into spirited debate. Novels wear dust jackets for a reason, preferring their own hermetic rarefaction. This is not a complete disparagement of interfaith dialogue. On the contrary, reasonable people of faith should probably keep engaging one another. For one thing, shared proximity complicates the launching of a Stinger missile. You might hit your pastor by mistake.

Comparative dialogue also diminishes our many jealous deities. All gods covet the role of Top God. Zeus veered between two base emotions—lust and jealousy—making him a shoe-in for CEO. A Maximum Leader by temperament, he chafed within the power-sharing pantheonic structure. Extreme-by-assertion ("there is only Me"), monotheisms are horrible goodwill ambassadors. But what can we do? Reintroduce animism? Audition Vestal Virgins? Vestal Virgin auditions accomplish nothing but spoiling the virgins.

For a time, it seemed like history might vex the old eschatologies right to sleep; secular humanism was on the rise, every suburban town had a Wiccan coven and Tom Cruise was at the top of the box office despite his Scientologist persuasions. But we've slipped back into a vicious struggle between the scorched-earth constituencies of Judaism (in its unyielding Zionist manifestation), Christianity and Islam—sort of an extremist-led game of chicken. Carelessly deployed language bears much of the blame here, as we've allowed ourselves to fall back on the old religious diatribes which, in turn, revive the old hatreds. If we could all just think of one another as what we really are—non-aligned assholes—and skip the religious invective altogether, the world would be a much safer place.

So whose nihilists are the baddest? That's the wrong question. Frankly all of them, together, draw from the same poisoned well. If religion really wanted to help, it might declare a moratorium on religious speech, silencing the many clerics who thrive on incendiary diatribe. Peace and quiet, at this moment in time, is perhaps the worthiest faith-based initiative.

Always with a keen eye for the sacred cow, journalist Christopher Hitchens mounts a spirited contrarian charge, bucking the media's tendency to de-pathologize the bad actors with religious palaver. Refusing to affix their abhorrent deeds to Islam's illustrious fifteen hundred year-old cultural tradition, Hitchens calls them what they really are: goddamned nihilists. Well, nihilists anyway. Here he is in a *LastSuperPower.net* interview:

> "Thus, any society run by [bin Laden] or people like him would keep on going bankrupt and starving itself to death, with no ready explanation of why this kept happening... Below even the bin Laden level, however, there are those who insist that they prefer death to life, and who really mean it. Suicide is not so much their tactic as their rationale: they represent a cult of death and they are wedded to destruction."

Precisely. Suicide bombings serve as their own rationale. Were they second-order activities, a tactic for example, palliatives might be devised. But mortally weary souls will not be assuaged when the mortal coil is everything that ails them. Hitchens should be applauded for sussing the existential abyss that looms behind the religious affectation. Indeed it benefits no one to Islamicize the villains nor Christianize the heroes: been there, done that—circa 1096. The real villains are the avowed enemies of culture and reason who champion death over life. Every tradition has them.

Jung suggested the age of the monotheistic gods would end only when they had accomplished their apocalyptic projects, something he viewed as an inexorable psychological process. Perhaps there have really only been two forces at play all along, reason and nihilistic destruction—Apollo and Dionysus. Champions of Reason and Culture from all religious and secular walks must vociferously disinvite their nihilist brethren. Let the latter petition the Earth without religious trappings, winning adherents on the merits of their own self-negating platforms. If such a campaign prevails, then we probably deserve them. But language, an adornment of culture, should not provide comfort to those who pursue oblivion and the cessation of humanity.

Until then, carnage at eleven.

GATHERING THE HERD

"The unfortunate truth is we're going to have to go in ... and put our people in the tough situation to save people who did not choose wisely. We'll probably do the largest search and rescue operation that's ever been conducted in the state of Texas,"—Andrew Barlow, spokesman for Texas Governor Rick Perry (R)

Like so many glorious contradictions in America today, the Hurricane Ike rescue effort provides the latest inducement not to probe too deeply the schism between wishful behavior (principle) and actions on the ground (reality.) People are suffering. This is true. Yet it begs asking: Why are lazy government bureaucrats endangering their lives to rescue rugged American individualists? These folks did not heed the New World Order's warnings to do the sensible thing. Perhaps it was a UN trap? The Trilateral Commission could easily have doctored those frightening hurricane trajectory videos. Photoshop can simulate choppy waters.

This is the pile-debt-up-for-another-day paradigm. We'll sanction the morons later—more likely from the diminished role of third-world banana republic status. The fact is, with every proud Texan plucked from his roof, rank ignorance scores another victory in America. When, one reckons, will the day of reckoning arrive for the tin-foil hat crowd? Why not let these folks test their survivalist skills for a few days? Where's George Bush to put a stop to this bleeding-heart public policy of saving the herd's stragglers? Why are we keeping them dry for another rainy day? Let Texas be Texas.

If America is hell-bent on being ignorant, then let it get about its business. But the world asks if it might hurry up and exit the world stage as its manifold errors redound to misadventure the world over. One hallmark of most successful civilizations is that rubes and provincials are encouraged to look upwards, aspiringly, if they are even addressed at all. In Karl Rove's America, the redneck is courted for his vote and exalted for his ignorance while the educated are held up for scorn and ridicule—mere effetes. In the current election, the operative Rosetta Stone is evolving towards whether the other guy can shoot and gut a caribou. This is a long way off from the arid abstraction of a credit crisis—though the latter may yet prove to be the bloodier enterprise.

Though it says little for the 21st century information age, the edification of ignorance should at least bode well for automaton-fascism. America may well don the brown-shirts before anyone else. The military industrial complex will make a fortune on the uniforms. True to form, the Toby Keith crowd keeps putting boots up everyone's asses while avoiding the thumbs firmly planted up their own. What politician wants to get booed at the next NASCAR rally?

As one economist noted wryly, just as there are no atheists in a foxhole, there are no libertarians in a financial crisis. The credit debacle is yet another example of ideological dereliction: we are privatizing gains and socializing losses. When ignorance is the ethos, intellectual consistency resigns as a major sticking point. The Hurricane Ike rescue efforts are only the most recent example of socializing stupidity and privatizing tough cowboy talk. When will these people ever get to walk their walk? How will they ever come to learn whether they even *have* a walk? Why does America continue to alienate courage from conviction? Who are we? Do we even know?

We know all politicians are Hugo Chavez in a crisis. That's how they get re-elected; by throwing money (not theirs) at their constituencies, however epically stupid the need may be. Ideological exactitudes are reserved for campaign bumper stickers. Then it's back to the real ideology: power and how to keep it. There is no expenditure too dumb if it can hold a congressional seat. Socialism wins elections by bailing out all manner of capitalist shenanigans while China—still run by the party of Mao—finances Yankee self-indulgence. Has the world moved into the post-ironic age?

Debt is a metaphor. There is a mountain of it. It keeps us from learning who we really are, what we in the present moment are capable of without recourse to the sweat of future generations. A $59 trillion debt liability makes every American a de facto hypocrite. No wonder we're coming to loathe one another. All speech slurs with a $59 trillion bar-tab. The best rhetoricians try but fail. The euphemism is, 'he makes us feel good about ourselves'. So does a good bartender. We are a den of thieves. Flush with near-worthless Fannie and Freddie agency paper, the world seems to be catching on.

Had Republican Texas Governor Perry denied on principle rescue services to those who rejected government-sponsored bus trips out of the area, it would have been a watershed event for two major reasons. First, it would have reconciled principle to political action. Second, it would have written Perry's political obituary as no politician of any stripe is expected to show temerity when his constituency requires government largesse.

People want their politicians to deviate from principle only when they want something. Championing consistency is sort of like asking Rev. Haggard to please refrain from procuring male prostitutes because it casts a pall over his Sunday morning exhortations, you know all that Christian-talk for which he was paid handsomely.

Dick Cheney, opponent of gay marriage has a gay 'married' daughter with, technically, an out-of-wedlock baby. Palin, spirited abstinence advocate, has an unwed teenage mother in her brood. Remember, it's a job, not a calling. What we do off the job is our own business. Is America real? Are we holding consummate performances up to the grim light of day when in 'reality' they should be left in the Great American Playhouse? Does anyone in America lead a life worthy of the term authentic anymore? $59 trillion makes such hypocrites of us all perhaps it's hardly worth pointing out hypocrisy anymore. Thieves pointing out thieves are no less thieves themselves. In an ethos that extols thievery, why even bother?

HOISTING YANK PETARD WITH BAUDRILLARD

Though it pains me to go all French philosopher in this, the aftermath of America's Silly Season, when Freedom Fries should still be the rage, I'm finding a Baudrillardian tact all but unavoidable. The American political process, and its convention spectacle in particular, has become a text-book hyperreality circus. There, I said it, *sacre bleu*! We have just lived through the concentrated excesses of a nation officially unhinged—and I don't mean Lyotard's hinged universe either. Or maybe I do. While the world does not send delegates, it dances at the Ball in a befuddled two-step of horror and fascination, though more horror of late. As has become tradition, it foots the bill as well.

Power is the adept wielding of imagery. As Bush and Company learned to our collective chagrin, when power relieves the enemy of his dark imaginings only to begin flexing its muscles in the likes of Fallujah and Tora Bora, keystone coppery and broken crockery can ensue. History will record that the past administration, led by bellicose non-combatants, possessed an overweening faith in its own tanks. It's always better to exude power than to conscript it into service where it runs the risk of appearing, well, rather weak. Therein lies the lost genius of the *show of strength*: no one gets hurt and you get your own way besides. Wise dogs know they are wagged surreptitiously by their tails.

In the age of the hyperreal, war constitutes abject failure; the dance of the hippopotami gone horribly awry. Convention planners are cleverer than Pentagon tacticians by at least half. The very real bid for power is assisted by erecting a false-reality of confetti, balloons and value-talk. If a term were coined, it might be aggressive artificiality. People are made to believe their votes, their consent, is the cost for buying into the euphoria. The consent itself is thus courted—and delivered—under false pretense. But the outcome is very real. Power is secured by those who mount the parade. This is not some giddy zero-sum game. The casino gets the money. The bells, whistles and ridiculous faux-ornate decor deliver the cash to the house's coffers. The crucial point is that the cash doesn't feel real while it's being handed over. The nefarious suspension of old-school practicalities through big-budget onslaughts is the key to the hyperreality gig. It also explains why the rich are getting richer at hyperspeed: they alone can advance the killer production budgets.

The real enjoys transport to the hyperreal for as long as it can pay to play. There is the illusory sense of real life's burdens being lifted after which you're sent home with empty pockets. The whole thing is a fetishized transaction wherein the consumer/voter is left tangibly diminished by the experience.

For those eccentric souls still nursing the homilies of ideology and belief, the float has long since passed you by. Righteous indignation has been replaced by what commentator Todd Peterson calls the 'fatuous taunt'. Power has become everything; blue versus red, red versus blue. Political rhetoric becomes a loose-fitting shirt easily changed from one skirmish to the next—if not shared between adversaries. An analogy would be the two teenage girls calling one another up to see what color jeans each will wear to school the next day. There's no need clashing if things can be ironed out in advance.

Commentator Leo Gerard has noted the dismay the other side displays when one of its positions is co-opted by the opposition. Why isn't there celebration over the meeting of the minds, unless of course it's all one big Monopoly game? You landed on my Park Avenue—now pay up sucker. The body politic should cheer grand rapprochements. Instead it bemoans the loss of a really good talking point.

In month one, Blue dings Red for 'lack of experience', to which Red protests mightily and counter-dings Blue for 'sexism'. In month two, the charges reverse as both sides perceive their relative vulnerabilities shifting, perhaps with two different candidates. Immediately the debate dissolves into recriminations of hypocrisy, each side citing the other's month-to-month inconsistencies. This kabuki dance is undertaken condescendingly enough for the benefit of the powerless who, it is thought, still retain vestiges of ideological constancy. The thinking is that, lacking power, they must be sustained by something—unshakable belief perhaps? Alas the plebes, increasingly insensate to the cascading reversals and counter-reversals of the powerful, begin to relinquish a firm grasp on the very notion of belief, not to mention the veracity of reality itself. The hyperreal shows itself as too deft and fleet-footed to be corralled by mere conviction. Power corrupts universally, from the top down.

As the society opts for stylized encounters, the American landscape drifts into a series of festering aftermaths: underwater mortgages, staggering national debt, sagging infrastructure, interminable wars. Alas collapsing bridges are uncooperative little buggers made of iron and concrete which is oblivious to political winds and utterly beholden to physics. Moreover they have every chance of toppling in good lighting as well as bad. The hyperreal is like a crack fix, far too seductive to be voluntarily relinquished—even as it compounds the dark overhang of a suspended reality (tragically a grim reality grows only grimmer as the fruitless bid to escape it is prolonged.) These darkening clouds heighten the desire to extend the hyperreal experience. Thus hyperreality digs deeper holes. But though the piper may dither he always get paid. Failing that, he steals your children whose futures have been mortgaged anyway through a bewildering array of structured financial products.

The Chinese and Middle Eastern sovereign wealth funds can forestall the reckoning for a time. But like a late-night poker hand where the pot has grown incommensurately high, all parties are getting nervous. This has been called the dollar trap, a permutation of the prisoner's dilemma. Everyone is pregnant with dollars. Thus the question becomes, who will bolt for the exit first? Rest assured one day soon, the casino boss will tap America on the shoulder and ask, in a respectful but firm voice, if the confetti bill can be paid.

This will not happen overnight. But it's more likely to months rather than years away. Right now, the world is still coming to grips with just how far it's bought into the American crack habit. The rug cannot be pulled climactically as this party is way too big to fail. After all the convention chairs were probably built in Taiwan and the microphone is Japanese. The world is a massive stakeholder in the largest Ponzi scheme in history. Indeed it thought we were building and buying houses for *habitation* when in fact we were manufacturing Freddie and Fannie paper for sale abroad and needed houses like so many Potemkin villages to rationalize the paper. Ten percent of all homes built in America since 2000 are empty. Taking up bricks and mortar, the hyperreal created a house of cards.

America's chief export is false-consumption. And the world responded, building crappy little sweat shops from Kuala Lumpur to Bangalore. If the curtain is allowed to be drawn back (and you can be assured third-world leaders are taking worried peaks right now), the shuttering of factories all over the world will create social unrest as has never before been seen. Indeed the dark side of globalization may manifest in a catastrophe of devastating simultaneity. Bullshit demand builds bullshit factories which lifted people, just barely, out of bullshit lives the whole world over. America has injected massive amounts of false promise (the globalization gig) into the hearts and minds of billions of people. Ponzi schemes tend to end in bangs, not whimpers.

Poker chips mean everything in the casino. Outside of it, they have all the intrinsic value of plastic milk containers. The hyperreality of the casino has swarmed the world economy. Indeed the casino is like the creature that ate Manhattan. If there is a Plan B, then it can only come from outer space as nothing on planet Earth remains exogenous. This is the claustrophobic nightmare of a fully integrated global economy.

If euros are frilly pieces of paper, dollars are frilly pieces of paper with a difference. Because global oil transactions are conducted primarily in dollars, dollars enjoy a certain exclusionary value, though hardly an intrinsic one. Think of dollars in the sense of cardboard boxes though with less utilitarian value. Exporters need cardboard boxes to ship their goods. Cardboard boxes are thus a *de facto* beneficiary of world trade. So are dollars. This is changing slowly.

Some doomsayers say the American economy is going to collapse. But economic collapse is a relative phenomenon. Compared to what? The rest of the world is going to collapse further. America, former eagle, will salvage pigeon-among-sparrows status which is exactly enough to retain its title as king among nations. But oh my, what a diminished kingdom it will sit astride. The whole world is on the hook, or is it on the brink? We will awaken from the American Dream together. At least it was a tasty jug of Kool-aid while it lasted.

A BARREL OF VERSE IS LIKE MONKEYS IN THE BANK

"I'm always struck by in-flight magazines as the example of culture's aesthetic anesthetic. Packaged in hermetic shrink-wrap and sandwiched between glossy photographs, the text here is bland but ideologically unmistakable—it takes the dream of the traveler and repackages it as the ultimate act of bourgeois desire: to possess distant realms, to transform all multifarious space into the flattened surface of the clear blue swimming pool or the green felt of a blackjack table."

I endorse Gunnar Benediktsson's despairing of the commodity effect's infiltration of art (in his on-line Editor's Note; March 2008 *5_trope* magazine), a durable Marxian trope if ever there was one. Everything is drenched in capital or *das capital* if you prefer. People say 'I love you' with the expectation of being loved back, which is less a plaintive appeal than a money back guarantee stamped on a *Whitman's Sampler*. These *quid pro quo's* are call option contracts promising the delivery of reciprocating emotion at a future date—passion in a barrel.

The present malady extends beyond mere macroeconomic phenomenon. For example, structured finance, the term, is an abomination. No one ever spills out of the pool in a paroxysm of synchronized swimming. How then can a flatland spawn a multi-verse?

Before the Laffer curve, there was Adam Smith, fellow Glaswegian and first-order moral philosopher—whose sphere of concern was human *congress* and only by inference its by-product, human *commerce*. Economist Eric Janszen hints at the symptom of the disease when he refers to our current quandary as the 'financialization' of America. I would suggest further that we now labor beneath a renegade financial superstructure that hangs above our heads like a sword of Damocles.

Once upon a time, finance was the duteous hand-maiden to industry, business and commerce; until it became unhinged, a thing-unto-itself. Now the old-school economy hangs in the balance—on the hook for trillions of dollars of purely financial obligations. If, as economist Michael Hudson argues, America needs to re-industrialize, how will the massive detritus from the financialization binge be addressed?

The moral compass has entered a reckoning phase. We are re-acquainting with the taut boundaries of value—at 4 am on the curb outside the bar. In the aftermath of a succession of burst bubbles, sober minds are right to ask how we managed to propel imputed value so far beyond any reasonable sense of the intrinsic. What hubris to believe the world would submit to the tin-soldiered exactitudes of algorithmic order. The originate-and-distribute 'debt model' was a moral abdication. To know thyself, one must know thy debtor too. Insurance should never become alienated from its insurable interest as it did in the credit default swap (CDS) market. The reckoning will be harsh indeed. Why should it surprise us that art was not spared?

Experimental art is attitude, the stalking of gesture over content. Perpetually interrogating the *status quo*, Benediktsson's experimental artist is always asking "what can [I] do about it." Keeping one step ahead of the shrink wrap engages most of his energies; acquiescence renders art 'shrunk'; diminished, shelf-bound. We'll get to the content later. The real question is did you actuate an escape?

A transactional veneer haunts the Internet poetry world: "I'll read your wares if you'll read mine." With each new Internet venue, we create a hermetically sealed Genius Camp, dilettantes bound together by tautological praise; good with any purchase. Like a stiff thumb in the eye, poetry should be better than that, though I concede there's little reason to expect it will. People should gush despite themselves rather than withhold approval for remuneration. A consumer weighs his exchange options as he mills about the mall, credit card at the ready. However poetry—the real stuff—blows past the shopper, striking the reader dead without dithering about until the check clears. If I can't detest your poem even as you adore mine, then the temple's money-lenders are managing the encounter.

Experimental art celebrates the act of commencing a departure—but as a traveler not as a tourist. The wallet is left behind. When the destination is a resort, no journey has been ventured, no abyss traversed. Tourism is a fatuous trap preventing hard-won gains; a Kodak gander at the ruins of *Machu Picchu* where, despite the sweltering heat of the third-world locale, no one breaks a sweat since the tour bus is air-conditioned. Visiting a resort is akin to moving from aisle three to aisle 11 in the local *Handy Mart*. From peanut butter to paper towels perhaps, but the operative irony is that no one leaves the store.

As Daniel Boorstin points out in his brilliant essay *"From Traveler to Tourist: The Lost Art of Travel"*, *tourist* was originally a term of derision. Even today, it evokes the pejorative. The luxury cruise lines deposit people in St. Thomas' Charlotte Amalie where they are urged not to stray far from the outlet malls. Apparently beyond the shopping enclaves it becomes dangerous for tourists. It's fair to ask, is their virginity preserved? Do they visit the Virgin Islands at all?

> "All destinations become 'destination resorts,' the experience of them so unmistakably transformed into their commodity form that we not only feel that we can purchase them, we know that by picking up this magazine, we already have."

Here, Benediktsson further implicates capitalism as a contagion. The world weathers this scourge presently as the western financial system, now universally embraced, teeters on the edge of the abyss. The casino is omnipresent. Immersed in everyday low prices, we have leveled all things with our cut-rate Midas touch—love, beauty, art, T-shirts. In our hands, everything takes on the meretricious aspect of mere inventory.

Ezra Pound warned of this all-eclipsing profanation where the "line grows thick". The pernicious commodity effect is greed's attempt to swarm all things: "with usura is no clear demarcation/and no man can find site for his dwelling." Alas the finest gold should resist purchase, or so we artists like to think. In a world-as-pervasive-marketplace, where is an artist to dwell?

Poets play kick-the-can with abandon. Bringing 'missionary zeal' to the project, they replace the dominant problem with a fresh impudence until, one day, it too is beaten into journeyman ploughshare, becoming cliché—commoditized language. For many, this inexorable wearing down begs the question, Why even bother? Because, living in the shadow of death, we live to postpone the shadow's ultimate victory. Of course death is never cheated. However there is a style of living, an attitude, which has us dancing just beyond the flames. An artist is one who has not yet assented to die. Like Orpheus, his journeys are harrowing life and death missions. He has the audacity to strike his own terms.

The alternative is nihilism—acceptance of Silenus' withering assessment (via Sophocles, later amplified by Nietzsche): "What is best of all is utterly beyond your reach: not to be born, not to be, to be nothing. But the second best for you is—to die soon." For all those who invite death into their lives, please conduct your transactions behind the graveyard and don't mind the children playing in the sunlit plaza, as for them summers have the feel of forevermore. Death will expand its province wherever it is allowed. We must choose from among the in-flight magazine's many tempting story lines, offering the currency of our lives. Anything less is a mere visitation.

FANNING THE EMBERS OF LOCALISM: THE LATE GREAT BROADCAST AFFILIATE SYSTEM

The television industry's longstanding practice of lowest common denominator-chasing has delivered on former FCC Commissioner Newton Minow's 'wasteland' in spades. Thus it's hard to imagine how any delivery scheme—-be it digital, analog or shadows cast on cave-walls—can fundamentally alter the qualitative nadir that comprises media content in America today. Buried in the hullabaloo over the great television digital cutover, then, is the more vexing question: *from what* and *to what* are we cutting over? Not much, it seems.

One wonders how the tenor of debate in America might have benefited had folks been raised on compelling science and history fare as opposed to *Gilligan's Island* and *Real Housewives of Orange County*. Tabulating the fearsome hours logged in front of the boob tube over the last half-century, we must conclude that the failure to conscript television as a medium of edification for the world's most influential society represents a lost opportunity of historic proportions. Oh well water under the bridge, and where's Iraq on a map again?

Then there is the greatest media vanishing act of all—from the fabric of our day-to-day lives (Note: the current spate of 'reality shows' does not count for any reality I'm familiar with.) Corporations are loath to acknowledge it but most living occurs, well, locally. Come to think of it living is a pretty individual affair when you get right down to it. And yet for economic reasons, the corporate media template is a reductionist one; that is, it seeks to consolidate and standardize programming in order to capture the most eyeballs at the lowest cost. Now admittedly there is a natural tension between what you or I want versus what the community as a whole desires. But at this critical juncture in the development of television especially, it bears asking: who besides corporations are being served?

Global interests promote global concerns. They are world-movers. That's what interests them. Who on Main Street clamors for fifteen venues of up-to-the-minute news on the Middle East? Presumably that would depend on how many viewers claim Tel Aviv or Beirut as their base of daily operation, which is to say no one in Peoria. Of far greater relevance to most Americans is the fate of their county's pending budget referendum or the local school construction debate. While perhaps not the stuff of heart palpitations, this news is increasingly being crowded-out by 'world-shaping events'. For those who fret washed-out bridges, school closings, oncoming cyclones, chemical spills, property tax initiatives, let them eat grass or heave Styrofoam bricks at Bill O'Reilly's smirking mug. Frankly my dear, Rupert Murdoch doesn't give a damn.

There are more profound cultural implications that redound from top-down reportage. Localism's polar opposite, globalization, can exert an alienating effect on people. In a crucial sense, we stop talking amongst ourselves. Globalism promotes incoherence. The tin foil hat crowd might offer this as yet one more plank in the New World Order agenda. If grass-roots communications can be curtailed, insurrection against the prevailing power structure can be quashed before it begins. Pitchforks acquire their business end one barn at a time. And was it one lantern by land and two lanterns by sea? In all the global hubbub, one can easily forget.

This brings us to another battleground on the globalism-localism front; between the national networks, by now *de minimus* offerings in larger media conglomerates, and their once-highly coveted partners, the local broadcast affiliates. While many of the latter are owned by the same global concerns, the majority of affiliates are essentially mom and pop operations. It bears noting also that not all local stations are affiliates, that is, 'affiliated' with a national network. But some 80% are. Imagine then waking to read the following quotes that appeared within days of each other just this past December (2008):

> "The entire broadcast model must change otherwise it will be like the newspaper business…" —Jeff Zucker CEO NBC Universal

> "Moving the CBS network to cable would be a very interesting proposition." —Leslie Moonves, CEO, CBS Corporation

There they were, the heads of two major networks, pondering aloud the continued efficacy of the broadcast model a mere two months before the February 17 cutover and after an estimated $13 billion digital upgrade investment. Where's the love? Indeed where's the shame?

But let's not shed too many tears for the hapless affiliates. That the latter's complicity in their own demise represents a classic example of zombie management disparages well-meaning zombies everywhere. Let's face it. Cable did not exactly creep up overnight. The migratory trend away from OTA broadcast has been underway for over twenty years. One must ask, what were they thinking, not to mention why embark on a $13 billion digital Maginot Line that promises to be obsolete almost upon inception?

According to FreeDTVPlus, since 1998 the market share of over the air (OTA) broadcast has cratered from 30% to 12%, with projections of 5% or less by 2010. Did the affiliates really think the inexorable migration of viewership to cable and direct broadcast satellite would not materially affect their market position? To be sure, an unknown (though it's thought a material) number of viewers pay for cable largely to improve the reception of their local TV channels. These folks might be thought of as broadcast fans 'in spirit' if not in practical effect. Yet delivery makes a difference. Shifting semantics helps to fog the picture a bit too. For example, what does one call ostensible 'broadcast' programming that reaches most homes via non-broadcast means? Even the terms themselves—*broadcasting, networks, et al*—are showing the strains of radically altered paradigms.

In the present moment of evaporating 401(k)'s, vanishing home equity and publically funded bank bonuses, we hardly needed dark TV's as a further populist rallying point. And yet there it is. Huey Long, where are you? Another old-school technology receiving a second look, perhaps a beneficiary of the recent economic funk, is dial-up Internet. Earthlink is reporting strong interest with its recent $2 price reduction to $7.95 per month Internet service. Echoing their OTA refrain, the pundits (no doubt ensconced somewhere in Manhattan) insist 'only' 9% of American households still rely on dial-up Internet. Unlike OTA, dial-up isn't going anywhere and may even get a second lease on life. It's worth pointing out that spam (the canned variety) and McDonald's value meals are enjoying a renaissance of sorts too. Deprivation encourages a myriad of low-tech options.

Indeed there remains a powerful public interest that continues to receive short-shrift. If, as the Association of Public Television Stations (APTS) suggests, fifteen million America households will awaken to blank screens when the cutover finally happens, then the Obama administration's sense of a looming populist backlash has real credence. APTS further suggests an implicit Universal Service mandate exists for free and ubiquitous television. And yet Public Broadcasting's member stations are on the digital forced march no less so than are their commercial counterparts. And what of the huge installed base of analog sets strewn about the average home for which the consumer cannot afford subscriber service? These sets threaten to become elaborate paper weights or dumb DVD monitors. Surely the lost consumer investment in these sets alone is staggering all by itself. Finally, between 1993 and 2008, cable rates have risen, according to the Consumers Union, by 53% over and above inflation. What types of rate increases should we expect in the future when consumer recourse to free broadcast television is eliminated? Even those with no interest in free TV should recognize the pricing discipline its presence exerts on the marketplace. Even more ominously, once free TV disappears and the affiliate structure withers away, it will never come back. There are no second chances.

To borrow from the late Tip O'Neil, news, like politics, is mostly local. With the collapse of local radio and the looming extinction of newspapers, the television network affiliates may soon become the only media game in town. There are a number of reasons why the affiliates are under siege at this time:

1. A projected 30% reduction in 2009 advertising revenues from 2008 due to deteriorating macroeconomic conditions and the migration of viewing audience to cable and Direct Broadcast Satellite (DBS) i.e. the lack of an originating audience.

2. Increasing economic pressures on national networks to 'go cable' (or DBS) and cut out the anachronistic 'redundancy' of the broadcast model altogether.

3. An overall erosion in TV viewership brought about by the Internet, broadband video streaming, video games, etc.

As the balance of this article has buried Caesar in earnest we should hasten, in the spirit of the Fairness Doctrine, to offer praise where praise is due. America needs the local stations. Indeed funny things happen on the way to extinction. Beyond its traditional and once-crucial role as the local licensee of national network programming, the affiliate structure has developed a formidable—and unparalleled—local news and programming presence. Of course much of this local programming is sustained by a network programming cross-subsidy which, among other things, provides 'lead-ins' to local shows (classic example, ABC Monday Night Football and the ABC local news whose ratings benefited greatly from immediately following the game.) What marquee programming that still originates on network television is being ardently courted by cable in a direct network-to-cable relationship—if not a cable end-run outright. As either scenario sidesteps the affiliate structure altogether, this cannot be good news for the former.

To be sure there are pockets of initiative out there—though nothing systemic or broad-based. For instance Weigel Broadcasting is teaming with Metro-Goldwyn-Mayer to provide old movies from the MGM catalog. Sinclair Broadcast Group is charging 'retransmission fees' to cable companies that carry their affiliate feeds. Already the networks are looking for a share of these proceeds. As CBS' Moonves said recently, "we feel we deserve a piece of it." Much of it *is* his network programming after all.

All need not be lost for the local stations. Indeed Virginia-based FreeDTVPlus claims to have a silver bullet to preserve free TV within the affiliate structure while fully utilizing the digital spectrum for multi-channel programming. The service involves combining it with the Internet to offer a bundled offering that competes actively with pay cable and DBS. From their website: "[We have the ability to] create, implement, maintain and upgrade a broadcast-centric DTV service platform that will enable the broadcasters to offer a multitude of new services to the home TV set."

Should the broadcast affiliate system fail to find a critical mass in a 'post-network' world, the local mantle will fall to cable TV's local access television. *Wayne's World* to the rescue. After all, what's left? One should be wary of placing too much faith in the future of local access. There is no great love for it either among the cable providers who must fund it or with the powerful who occasionally weather its citizen-fueled diatribes. As Jim Flynn, former BOD President of Virginia's Fairfax Public Access says, "that's why cable television wants to close down public access. It drains profits and the local government doesn't want it—it could upset the apple cart."

One can easily imagine a politician asking, "why should I subsidize a platform for pretenders to my throne? Isn't that the media equivalent of slitting my own throat? Let them go out and sell their souls like I had to, one corporate contributor at a time." Thus the well-connected's battle-cry may indeed be "local schmocal." After all these ambitious souls want to graduate to the world stage and get on CNN. Until then county dog-catcher will have to do. Our communities are their stepping-stones. We would be foolish to think otherwise. In short, local access television has no well-heeled advocacy. *We The People* are its natural constituency.

But are *We The People* aware of the stakes, and frankly, do enough of us even care? Localism must be championed at the grassroots level because localism *is* the grassroots level. No one will swoop down from on-high to save our bully pulpits. In this debate especially, politicians rank among the least of our friends. Nor are their enablers, media moguls, all that far behind.

WAR FOOTING

ABSENCE MAKES THE HAWK GROW STRONGER

By fortuitous circumstance, the call to arms is a bugle call few of us will ever need rise to. For this, we are indeed blessed. Too young for Vietnam, too old for Iraq, I am one such grateful non-combatant. But there is a group of unconscientious objectors for whom personal bravery seems to sprout with gray hair. Breathtaking hypocrites, they promulgate war on the backs of others even as they themselves evade combat when their own number is called. Today's Iraq plays fool to such a war.

Wobbly knees are not the exclusive province of war. Indeed they can be found in the most innocuous schoolyard tussles or bar-room brawls. Example? A fight is on the verge of breaking out, fisticuffs seem inevitable. One person shrinks back from the conflict and the fight fizzles. This is a good thing. Cooler heads have prevailed. Or so it seems.

Then a strange thing happens. No sooner does the imminent danger pass than the faltering combatant 'finds his voice' and begins screaming "lemme at 'em! lemme at 'em!" If he's lucky, there's a cadre of friends to hold him back while he performs his averted-war-dance. Of course by this time, his opponent is well out of earshot, something our erstwhile hero calculates marvelously. In a less enlightened era, such behavior might be called cowardice, camouflaged of course by the face-saving denouement. Much to a nation's great cost, such flailing can be suppressed for years until an Oval Office plays host to the Monday morning bravado.

Cowardice. In all likelihood, modern psychiatry has a more palatable term, enshrined in an acronymic 'syndrome', and cap-stoned with a pharmacological happy-pill to make everyone feel better about themselves. But in a bygone, pre-clinician era, ignoble episodes could forever besmirch a man's reputation and honor, causing him to slink away from public life altogether. In fact, a Victorian gentleman could find himself so ostracized even his psychiatrist would decline his calls. Dire indeed. Today, the shamed-faced simply aspire to higher office—and with an odd political advantage to boot.

America is the land of second acts. But with all due respect to Dr. Jack van Impe and the Rapturists, George W. Bush may be answering to an even higher calling when he talks of being "re-born". Forget the Hereafter. Bush needed Evangelical Christianity so he could face Dad again in the here-and-now. The patriarchal breach thus repaired, it was a quick dash to the Texas Governorship and then onto the apogee of his dynastic birthright.

But make no mistake. There is an unscratchable itch in a dark recess of Bush's patrician soul. Vietnam remains his war-of-first-order. Neither Richard Nixon's 'peace with honor' nor Billy Graham's one-on-one ministrations could ever absolve such an intensely private abdication. The storied nature of political dynasties is such that private failings often require public extirpations. Vietnam, George Bush's tragic flaw, presages our current national nightmare like a long-lost bookend.

Iraq is at least in part, an Oedipally-inspired second act, albeit seasoned with a dash of Armageddon. It is the boy who, afraid to jump into the pool, stops the world to redress his initial failure of nerve. WMD's are merely the pedestrian excuse Bush offers for his second chance at the deep end. You see, the reason was never really *the reason*, if you get my reasoning. Everything was about jumping in again.

Stopping the world to make Mom swoon means good men and women must die. So let's hope Barbara picks her favorite guy real soon 'cause my copy of *Left Behind* is getting pretty dog-eared, and the troops are stretched thin. On the chance Barbara's subscription to *Liberty* is still current and she's soliciting second opinions over this Freudian impasse, George Sr. gets my vote, hands down.

Frequently labeled a Presidential wimp, George Sr. was a bona fide WWII war hero. Pardon an Orwellian segue, but everyone *knows* war heroes are wimps. And if you don't, well comrade, there's a Room 101 with your name on it. The recently departed Ronald Reagan, Star Wars aficionado and Cold War warrior, served in the show biz wing of the WWII effort. This means the closest he ever got to blood was stage ketchup. Of course the image makers assured us Reagan 'exuded strength'. George McGovern, decorated—and stoically reticent—WWII B-24 pilot war hero, was decisively painted into the wimp corner by Nixon's burgling band of brothers. John Kerry, decorated war hero, recently used the unfortunate adjective "sensitive" to describe his differing philosophy on prosecuting an effective war. Dick Cheney, draft dodger and hawk, seized upon this rhetorical gaffe to reveal Kerry's inherent wimpiness. And let's not recount on a full stomach the character assassination Vietnam paraplegic Max Cleland suffered at the hands of his political nemeses, arguably the armchair hawks' most despicable moment. In all manner of battlefields—real and political—character, or the lack thereof, always reports for duty, sir. My, how the hawks resemble doves and the doves, hawks. But then, war is peace, right Winston? Or is everyone simply looking like the pigs they are?

It's time to uncork a new term: asynchronous bellicosity. Hopefully, the APA will see fit to list it as a bona fide mental disorder. Symptoms? The farther a non-combatant recedes from direct personal harm, the more combative he becomes. Conversely, the farther a combatant recedes from direct personal harm, the more circumspect he becomes about sending others into harm's way. Perhaps non-combatants can still luxuriate in war fantasy-glorification while the real-dealers can no longer countenance John Wayne in Green Beret get-up without suffering post-traumatic flashbacks. Whatever the reason, The Home of the Brave is increasingly being governed by the Un-brave Who Chose to Remain Home.

In moral terms, it's a hop, skip and a jump from chicken to corporatist/statist pigeon. So it's fair to ask whether our current sitting co-President Dick Cheney is acting, first and foremost, as committed civil servant or as Halliburton Chairman Emeritus. Can a blind trust swim? I for one can't tell. But I am reminded of Ayn Rand's admonition in *The Roots of War*: "The actual war profiteers of all mixed economies were and are of that type: men with political pull who acquire fortunes by government favor, during or after a war—fortunes which they could not have acquired on a free market."

Not that I begrudge our fighting men and women their $300 daily meal stipends care of Cheney's old employer. If the troops are truly dining in royal splendor, I'm a happy prole. But at some price-point you're gonna hit a culinary wall with MRE's.

So Iraq is George's second crack at Vietnam, and perhaps Cheney's pot of gold. Fortunately for Bush, Vietnam is so far down the Ho Chi Minh Trail of history that not even a stray Viet Cong bullet can hit him now. This means that, despite his rebirth as Warrior King, he'll never be required to rattle his saber other than from behind a desk. And whose heart didn't sink when George declined Saddam's pre-war challenge to hand-to-hand combat, mano a mano? Perhaps he isn't re-born after all, and it's the same Ole George, out to save nothing but his own skin. Such cynicism would no doubt cause the Rev. Pat Robertson, Korean War dodger, holy heart palpitations. So I'll refrain from further inquisitions.

Another casualty of the modern age is the notion of *noblesse oblige*. Far from obligating today, nobility, or at least privilege, seems only to open a floodgate of safe harbors. Rand instructs again: "If an heir is equal to his money, it serves him; if not, it destroys him." Judging by the war-time records of Bush Sr. and Jr., even in the same family, some are more equal than others. I acknowledge this verdict may be somewhat prejudicial as a complete record of Bush Jr's National Guard service was unavailable at the time this article went to press. One man's two-act pantomime is another's Waterloo. As it happened, George W. Bush's second war was Pat Tillman's first—and last. Let it be noted that, on the auspices of his grim occasion, Tillman rose, deliberately and courageously. The operable old-school terms are duty and sacrifice. In the wake of Pat Tillman's death, the general upper-crustine chorus was one of incredulity. After all, here was a young man 'with everything going for him'. And yet, he 'went patriotic', buying the whole God-and-country thing when he could just as easily have bought a fleet of Lamborghinis. Brave? Heroic? Dangerously naive? Avariciously bankrupt? Where was his moral calculator, his calculated clarity? More alarming still, how did his character manage so thoroughly to cloud his judgment? What a senseless waste of future cash flows. In their musings, the ruling class betrayed contempt and disdain for the sacrifices of the less-well-connected. The tenor of the Tillman retrospective was palpable: "War is for dead-enders."

Such an extraordinary young man as Pat Tillman could easily have become the progenitor of a fresh, new political dynasty. Trouble is, would Tillman have had the stomach for modern politics? After all, he might have faced a phalanx of reconstructed, recriminating hawks, since (if recent history is any judge) there was every chance of him returning home a committed dove. War has a way of doing that, even to the best of us.

WAR STORIES

"...Now all my lies are proved untrue
And I must face the men I slew.
What tale shall serve me here among
Mine angry and defrauded young?"
—Epitaphs of War (1914-18), "Dead Statesman", Rudyard Kipling

Leading up to the mid-term elections, the Bush administration's portrayal of the Iraq project had gone stupendously momentous. In his 9/11 Five Year Anniversary Speech, George Bush described the conflict in startling terms: "the early hours of [the] struggle between tyranny and freedom." No longer *merely* an inter-civilizational battle, the conflict had morphed into a struggle for civilization itself. With the war faltering, the war of words bellows at compensatory volume. The enterprise is widely acknowledged as a failure. Strange then how its scope hurtles ever outward and the hour of the day—like a stopped clock—is still early. We're being plied with cheap wine to wash down a steady diet of mission creep as our leaders struggle to forestall recognition of their own failings. This procrastination is abetted by fresh levels of grandiose imagery and language.

Witness the latest conniptions in Washington DC over whether Iraq has indeed slipped into a civil war. A recent Washington Post article ("The Wagging of 'Civil' Tongues", Dana Milbank, 'Washington Sketch' column, August 22, 2006) wryly acknowledges the fierce war of words underpinning the war itself: "Facing a linguistic insurrection, the administration rallied its semantic defenses. 'They have sectarian differences, and some of those are violent,' Secretary of State Condoleezza Rice said. 'It's not civil war.'" Clearly words still matter to the powers-that-be.

Beginning his own redemptive, albeit rhetorical, process toward extracting the ideal of war from the ensuing carnage this ideal habitually spawns (i.e. atrocities, torture, unintended geopolitical consequences, social collapse, etc.), conservative soul-searcher Andrew Sullivan recently posed this question on his blog: "Was the [Iraq] project always doomed or did the execution doom it?"

It's unlikely civilization as we know it will give up the ghost on the strength of this administration's misadventures. However ask a Carthaginian or a Trojan, if you can find one, and he may tell you that civilizations can turn on a few ill-judged battles. More often than not though, when leaders resort to mighty-civilization-talk, it's a smokescreen aimed at concealing more parochial foibles: ignorance, surprise, miscalculation, incompetence, confusion. No doubt America's notion of civilization will survive the Iraq debacle, even as nearly three thousand of its sons and daughters will not.

As for Sullivan, an early proponent of the war, he is beginning to carve the ledge upon which many of his fellow squawks (armchair hawks) will, in due course, be arranging their seat cushions. You can almost hear the gathering symposium of sedentary voices as they warm up in the punditocracy's many Green Rooms: "we supported the war, not its abysmal prosecution." Ah, the finer points of valorous debate. Can't we please ship all impossibly eloquent warmongers to Fallujah?

Conservative face-saving aside, Sullivan's question—while attracting perhaps a surface interest—never entertains more than a surface reality. That's because it's a rhetorical tempest wrapped in a right-wing tizzy fit.

So what did come first, the dead chicken or the rotten eggs? The proof is offered in the scale of the early planning. Not even former Secretary of Defense Donald Rumsfeld would have seriously proposed a 130,000-troop force-level for the purpose of prevailing in a veritable battle for the universe. As for the evolution of war-time propaganda, one need only follow the rhetorical swell.

In the Iraq War especially, a cogent narrative must now contend with a time span of previously unimagined duration—at least by the standards of pre-war rhetoric. That is why, with most benchmarks already historical fait accompli (an Iraqi constitution, a free election, the capture of principal villains) the time-line-as-hopeful-predictor-of-events has reached its terminus. With the storyline all used up, the present moment becomes infinitely more perilous. There is nothing to which imminent arrival can lay claim, much less claim victory. We are now in an interminable phase of War Time where the vagaries of time itself spool out into the uncharted void.

Once upon a time, there was virtual unanimity among the powerful that time was on their side. By commencing the war on a date-certain, the implicit presumption was that all subsequent events would submit themselves to an executive day planner. As Bush assured in his September 14, 2001 National Cathedral speech, "this conflict...will end in a way, and at an hour of our choosing." Such was the unabashed certitude of the last remaining superpower. Indeed the hubris was palpable as the main players offered predictions in the run-up to hostilities:

1. February. 7, 2003, Secretary Rumsfeld, to U.S. troops in Aviano, Italy: "It is unknowable how long that conflict will last. It could last six days, six weeks. I doubt six months."

2. March 4, 2003, Air Force Gen. Richard Myers, chairman of the Joint Chiefs of Staff, at a breakfast with reporters: "What you'd like to do is have it be a short, short conflict...Iraq is much weaker than they were back in the '90s," when its forces were routed from Kuwait."

3. March 16, 2003, Vice President Cheney, on NBC's Meet the Press: "I think it will go relatively quickly...(in) weeks rather than months."

What a difference a war makes. One of the salutary effects of the media age is that wars, particularly incoherent ones, must contend with a rear-guard action from a voracious twenty-four-hour news cycle. Given a sprawling gap of time, all manner of earnest truth-tellers are drawn to the microphone: retired generals with axes to grind, arm-chair media quarterbacks, inevitable second-guessers, officious micro-managers, conflicted soul-searchers, disgruntled former officials, grieving survivors, emboldened journalists and on-the-ground bloggers.

Time inflicts its own grave wounds upon a stalled war effort. Had the war been prosecuted expeditiously—as per plan—a multitude of sins would have been buried forever beneath mounds of confetti and ticker tape. To the victor go the spoils of composing history. As it is, there's been three years of chimerical WMD caches, Abu Ghraib atrocities, the Woodward trilogy, John Murtha and Cindy Sheehan, a seeming drip-drip of the inevitable bad news that any war will produce—when afforded ample time.

A war's duration molds its final complexion. The rhetorical equivalent of cosmetic enhancement, this war has enjoyed its share of thematic nips and tucks. Words carry their own peculiar power. You want to recruit an endless stream of Islamo-fascists? Play into their grandiosity by invoking them as a movement worthy of the attention of the United States. With tragic irony, it may be the sheer rhetorical effrontery of this particular war that drags the world into a war between civilizations. Think of it, a war that sparked a successor war. Not so absurd, perhaps; the seeds of WWII were firmly planted in the aftermath of WWI.

Reaching back in the annals of interminable conflict, we find the words of Abraham Lincoln from his Second Inaugural Address strangely prophetic, if not a bit chilling: "Neither party expected for the war the magnitude or the duration which it has already attained. Neither anticipated that the cause of the conflict might cease with or even before the conflict itself should cease."

In a voice thick with fatalism and drained of hubris, Lincoln by 1865 could nonetheless continue to say, quite plausibly, that slavery was the root cause of the Civil War. But what if the Union Army had found no slaves upon crossing the Mason-Dixon Line in 1861? Would the conflict have raged on for another four years? Rhetoric has its tactical limitations. Today we face the unsettling task of fighting a war whose cause seems to have vanished in the midst of battle. A war with no discernible *causi belli* is an illegitimate war, *prima facie*. So why didn't we leave yesterday? We remain to ameliorate the effects of going there in the first place. We remain because leaving might further aggravate the wound caused by our arrival. We remain because we are there.

There are political fortunes and careers to think about. The frantic dissembling of our leaders as they struggle to save face and power is, regrettably, the nature of that particular beast. Self-preservation is a first-order political instinct. At this advanced stage of the conflict, honest men and women have a duty to demand of their politicians: what are we fighting for? This message was articulated in the results of the mid-term election.

Not surprisingly, the recent amplification of the war's stated aims was timed to coincide with the mid-term election cycle. Tasked with attempting to preserve a majority, Karl Rove was almost certainly the architect. For one thing, it smacks of the 'clash of culture' clarion call so often used to incite what Sullivan calls the Christianist wing of the Republican Party. Incumbent legislators—frankly of both parties—needed a rhetorical barricade, a phrase to hang their hats. No doubt civilization would be better served by throwing *all* the bums out. At least fresh bums have the leeway to break with bad prior policy. It remains to be seen just how spirited an opposition the new Democratic majorities in Congress will provide. Both parties are equally beholden to Zionist interests, at least as much as they are to the will of the American people.

This is not to say that the original Iraq plan lacked for ambition, even as it was peddled to the general public as a little ole WMD scavenger-hunt. The Neo-conservatives, students of elitist-extraordinaire Leo Strauss who famously endorsed deceiving the masses for the purpose of accomplishing the Greater Good, set out to accomplish in Iraq the first leg of a Middle-East Marshall Plan—by itself, no small task, though substantially less ambitious than, say, a battle for the soul of world-civilization.

The neo-conservative blueprint can be found in the eerily prescient Statement of Principle written in 1997 under the auspices of the Project for a New American Century (PNAC). Practically wistful in its tone for "some catastrophic and catalyzing event—like a new Pearl Harbor" with which to cement American resolve for Middle East interventionism, the Statement has become the Rosetta Stone for conspiracy theorists everywhere. If PNAC didn't explicitly coordinate the 9/11 attack (a thought this writer simply cannot entertain), then surely they provided the karmic framework for such a 'fortuitous' tragedy to ensue. One has only to look at the military adventurism commenced over the last five years under the ostensible banner of 911 to realize that full advantage was taken. Does it matter frankly whether the conspiracy was overt or implicit given the subsequent chain of events?

Iraq was to be the oil-rich, self-financing and democratized beachhead for this enterprise. Horrible execution in Iraq has surely shelved any large-scale transformative Mid-East plan for at least another generation, if not another century. Given the demographic realities pressing down on Israel, this delay may indeed prove fatal to that outflanked entity.

As the tactical miscues mounted—driven largely by Rumsfeld's 21st century (read: woefully inadequate) military force—the rhetoric had no choice but to grow to match the ever-widening scope of the fiasco. Thus it's in Rummie's tactical quagmire that the etymological roots of our current hyperbolic struggle for the soul of the universe can be traced.

The bad Greek play that is Iraq has a flawed character for every palette. In the flash of a U.N. Powerpoint presentation, Colin Powell became our era's Neville Chamberlain, an apologist for epic, if not outright willful, geo-strategic miscalculation. Senator Carl Levin characterized Powell's lapse in good counsel to the President as a complete "abdication." For Powell anyway, the rehabilitative gears are in full swing. We learned recently that he was merely a loyal soldier serving at the pleasure of his President. But what was a tin soldier doing in the role of our nation's Diplomat-in-Chief, a position more suited to the wiles of a Metternich? It pays to recall that Powell, the most popular Republican figure in 2000, was selected to the Bush cabinet on the strength of his electoral appeal. Whether he was offered the right seat is a matter of debate. This is not to impugn Powell's competence; merely to say his selection was preeminently a political one.

Cheney wears many hats: corporatist, ideologue, Beltway bandit, war profiteer, Shylock. No doubt a potent enabler of the war effort with his proximity to the President, he seems more a synthesizer of various pro-war interests, than a Prime Mover. Though I readily confess this is pure conjecture on my part.

Relative influence notwithstanding, Cheney's formidable arrogance is handily eclipsed by that of his former boss, Don Rumsfeld. An unbowed technocrat of no great ideological persuasion, Rumsfeld was clearly cut from the Robert McNamara-MBA-wunderkind cloth. Awash in hubris and repeating Hitler's mistake, he endeavored to prosecute two fronts simultaneously. The easy one, he thought, would be subduing the Baathists; the harder one would be disabusing the Pentagon's old-school Army brass of their penchant for large scale 'boots-on-the-ground' warfare. As it turned out, neither adversary proved a particularly easy opponent, or is it that both enjoyed an accidental alliance, deriving advantage from combined strength?

Rumsfeld had to fight the Baathists (boss' orders). But he could easily have postponed an internecine turf battle for a more propitious time. In his outsized ambitions, Rumsfeld betrayed the fatal flaw of so many would-be heroes: he thought himself too clever—by about half-a-war. The real tragedy is that, to pay for Rummie's overreach, America may well have to lose. Twice.

History may well tap Rumsfeld as the Kaiser Wilhelm—or is it the mad Captain Ahab?—of the Iraq debacle, with copious assistance from a bevy of second-mates. The White Whale never changes: it's always existential dread, and of course inexhaustible terror.

Indeed the nation finds itself on a bloody, strategically unmoored, treadmill fueled by arrogance and denial. Or, as former diplomat Richard Armitage characterized the current vacuous circle: "We've got to have more men fall to honor the memories of those who have already fallen."

Armitage's loopy logic echoes the grinding banality and capriciousness of WWI so grimly captured in Erich Remarque's seminal war novel, *All Quiet on the Western Front*: "A word of command has made these silent figures our enemies; a word of command might transform them into our friends." Who today possesses the courage to end a war that lacks the internal logic to end itself?

In WWI, fear for the consequences of cessation without victory created its own rationale, prolonging the carnage beyond any reasonable 'military objectives'. A refusal to 'cut and run' can be a facet of character, provided it doesn't descend into stultifying inertia. It must never substitute for a strategy. Yet isn't it being touted today as precisely that, a strategy?

Of course when wartime enters an interminable phase, the optimal time for ending the madness is always sooner rather than later. Capping the innate absurdity of WWI, an armistice was arranged for the 11th hour of the 11th day of the 11th month of 1918. Poetic logic suggests a perfectly logical cessation date for the current war: the 11th day of the 11th month of 2008, 11:00 pm sharp. That would be ninety years to the hour after the Great War's end, and seven days before the election of a new President. For those with a more meaningful end-date, the world is all ears.

HUBRIS AND ITS PERENNIAL NEMESIS, WAR

"When we understand that slide, we'll have won the war." —General Stanley McChrystal, Commander, U.S. Forces, Afghanistan

In this, the sesquicentennial of the American Civil War, we find ourselves vexed anew with 21st century military slogs. Abraham Lincoln's essential exegesis on war, the *Second Inaugural Address*, cautions us with prophetic urgency:

I cannot read it without a shiver running down my spine. This is Lincoln at his cryptic best, scrupulously avoiding the taking of sides, even as the side he leads seems poised for imminent victory. No doubt there are elements of Lincoln the astute politician as well, laying the early groundwork for his post-war role as peacemaker and conciliator.

Contrast this Lincolnian *gravitas* with the modern era's bounty of rhetorical punch-lines ('bring 'em on'), clear-and-present phantoms, weapons of mass fiction—all suggestive of conflicts initiated by Man as opposed to Just Wars ordained by God (as helpfully explicated in various Augustinian-Aquinian writings.) Euphemistic clues are the *police action* and the *authorization for the use of force*—parliamentary half-measures that more suggest political generalship than a charge up San Juan Hill. How interesting that one must go back to WWII to find a war formally declared by the U.S. Congress. How damning that in this, the military-industrial age, no conflict has risen to formal war status since the onset of said age. Parenthetically, I am reminded of Ayn Rand's description of war profiteers; their success derives not from martial imperative but rather government favor and cronyism: "Statism needs war; a free country does not."

Given the theological dimensions of Lincoln's remarkable speech, there is little doubt he saw God's imprimatur on the American Civil War. He deftly counter-poses the inscrutable Creator with Man's feeble, hubristic attempts to conscript the latter to his cause. As Lincoln points out rather sardonically, both sides cannot possibly be prosecuting God's will. For one thing, there's the not-so-small detail of each worshipping the same God. Surely Yahweh speaketh not with forked tongue?

In truth, war more resembles a *deus ex machina*, oblivious to all sides, descending upon Man and leaving him little choice but to wage it. Invariably, rationales are devised. Rallying cries, banners and earnest reconstructions of *causa belli* ensue. These various human rationalizations represent futile attempts to assign scrutability to what is ultimately an inscrutable endeavor.

The ways of God resist the pale calculus of human reason: "All dreaded it, all sought to avert it…and the war came." There is a deterministic inevitability to the 'coming' of the war. For all their pretensions as agents of the first order, men are mere instrumentalities. And yet, Lincoln invokes his own interpretive prerogative, divining that God's sensibilities are so offended by the evil of slavery, that it MUST be the root cause: "All knew that this interest [slavery] was somehow the cause of the war."

Lincoln is not infallible. On a separate occasion he laments, "If I could save the Union by freeing the slaves, I would; if I could save the Union by not freeing the slaves, I would." That Lincoln might be guilty of occasional inconsistency serves only to confirm his own human status. The power of this particular speech is undiminished. Alas its lesson remains largely unlearnt.

We see this persistently hubristic impulse on grand display in the Pentagon's by-now legendary *Powerpoint* slide on Afghanistan. Surely only God Himself could preside over—let alone comprehend—this panoply of causes, counter-causes, insurgent motives, imputed responses and strategic half-nelsons. The chart reeks of Faustian triumphalism; the notion that if we can only get our hands around the totality of human motivations, then those twin vagaries—Fate and God's Will—might be harnessed and subdued. Where, in this intricate mosaic that practically screams the imprimatur of think-tank, do we account for the vaunted fog of war? Had the neo-cons only read less Leo Strauss and more Lincoln, imagine what could have been avoided.

Fate is the province of God, not the Joint Chiefs of Staff or, God forbid, Microsoft. Since time immemorial, the mightiest kings have met their match in Ozymandias' "lone and level sands." It is hard to imagine technological innovations or Halliburton usurping Shelley's poetic vision.

The grand illusion of control, abundantly evidenced by the Pentagon's assiduous arrows and tactical zones of influence, is a conceit that Lincoln brilliantly exposed nearly 150 years ago. How sad that his successors failed to heed this crucial lesson of history. In the most chaotic endeavor of all, war, human mastery is a pipedream. A five-year veteran of war's maddening ebbs and flows, Lincoln would offer only this on the eve of almost-certain military victory: "With high hope for the future, no prediction in regard to [the war's outcome] is ventured."

A healthy trepidation—as opposed to a bloodless, diagrammatic certainty—is the hallmark of wisdom. The only war-cry worth its salt? "Get thee behind me, hubris."

SUSPICIOUS WHITE POWDER: BAD ACTORS IN AN AGE OF BAD EQUALITY

"An emancipated society... should rather point to the bad equality of today, the identity of film interests with weapons interests, and think of the better condition as the one in which one could be different without fear."—Theodor Adorno, (from Minima Moralia, Aphorism 66, 1951)

Sold on pastoral endings and the coy backward glance, America, the world's autist, insists on its own terms: civil war, insurgency, pockets of resistance, dead-enders, a few bad eggs. But the world, sold on nothing in particular, gives nothing up.

This clash of civilizations resounds in warring factions that seek to define war on another man's turf, using sound bites market-tested in a Beltway think tank. Columns of contractors shield millions from the whites of another man's eyes. For this, steep tribute is paid, feeding a shell-game of letterheads. Drones are the crystallizing emblem, the empty casings of outsourced character; the actor who emerges, unscathed, slathered in movie-blood, claiming to do his own stunts. Unmanned wars loom like the next brave frontier claiming the New American Century while freeing-up the best and brightest for movie-lot tours of duty. Zipperless fucks in impregnable titanium tanks are every techie's wet dream. But is this bold embrace of absence a clandestine departure?

Even in its storybook heart America knows that armed conflict, left unattended, can spoil the most carefully-conceived *mise en scene*. Hundred Year Wars ravage a filmic sensibility. Eisenstein, Stalin's docile chronologist, abolished them in favor of the flashpoint. Given the shifting paradigm of today's infotainment complex, no studio will bankroll a century. Editors practice their own brand of fascism in the dark-room after a long hard day of shooting. Movies are what a culture's history aspires to, particularly when the Pentagon offers its full cooperation. Done well, a Great Lie can hold back an accounting of biblical proportions—provided the right permissions are obtained. The military complex opens up like a wine cellar to patriotic directors known to embrace a certain military ethos. Goebbels was careful never to curb Riefenstahl's access to the vast storehouse of Nazi paraphernalia.

This wealth of cherished falsehoods emboldens homegrown firebrands, our own Aryan fanatics, to vote with their skin for cinematic victory and its easy accoutrements: ticker tapes, chastened foes given over to liberty, a zealot's creeping temperance, white flags, prison swastikas, ceremonial pens. But every beachhead must contend with fresh configured sands. Nothing from this busted carnival ride will ever trod the hallowed ground of Omaha Beach again. Spielberg rode that moment into the terminus of an Oscar sunset.

In the dead of endless summer, some fierce circle completed itself and split tinsel town without reporting to its agent. John Wayne owned Okinawa. But his Waterloo was Vietnam. If victory, in the American sense, is an American invention, how will we retrofit its thirst for glory to this dull ironic age? Who will rise like a thief with stolen medals? What new false idol with matinee looks will lead the charge? Irony devours role models. But somehow our nightmares must be vexed back to sleep. Dick Cheney, hunkered down in an undisclosed location with a stack of John Ford movies, cannot turn back the clock alone.

So where are today's paragons? Today's returning kids, baptized in PTSD and asymmetric force, are left struggling alone with jihadists hell-bent on dreams of paradise. Rummy cries mummy for Paris Peace Talks. But deliberation betrays the secularist's chief mission of staying alive, a telling sign of weakness. At least the Commies manned the leeward side of the dialectic, rearranging bourgeois deck-chairs while endlessly rehashing the same five year plan. Now there was an enemy that could be counted on for old-school brinksmanship.

There's only one shell-game in this enemy's agenda: peace-through-rigor-mortis. At least there is broad consensus on the subject of eternity: From some noxious pit of fire, the vanquished will petition the sneering top-God even as the larger universe screams its ambivalence at the many bad actors who speak in its name. Show us oh Lord a demiurge not deserving of a swift kick in the ass, and we will embrace his ineffable wonderment, verily we say.

Blame the double feature, but America sat and watched too long, out-sourcing courage to the shadowy world of lucrative contracts. Our appointment with death and dismemberment seems interminably deferred. Cameras are forbidden to probe the flag-draped secrets of the Trojan horse in Dover AFB's back-lot. No General worth his chest-ware dares visit for fear of seeing his own crestfallen stars on the gurney, the gold caked in rust. Learning to walk again challenges the canon of the suburban multiplex. Prosthetics ring hollow until some consummating vision slams the table with clenched fist.

The whole thing smells like napalm in the morning, the ruinous aftermath of a defeated worldview. Iraq is that vaguely familiar character actor sprouting six degrees of tentacles. Every failure needs a locus of evil, a sinner to be scourged from the bully pulpit.

Truth is always where the bombs fall. There is nothing even slyly ironic about a missile in your kitchen. But this is the cost of facing an unscripted enemy. Waves of nausea, no doubt clandestine shipments from Syria, attack—only to fade back into ineffable night when the Cavalry of Zion thunders into town. Irony, hardly a seminal force, churns out anti-heroes like aging rock stars on their third farewell tour. Jessica Lynch's fiercest battle was stateside with the soldiers of propaganda. Pat Tillman, of Rushmore jaw and raw manipulated courage, was shot from behind by a jealous comrade who failed to make the high school JV football team. Tillman's hooded assailant, probably a black man, nursed his own domestic wound: a shrinking factory floor that made his trigger-finger itch, forcing him onto the grassy knoll of paranoia.

Americans cringe at the horrendous opportunity cost of friendly fire, money being the last pill-box on the hill—impregnable to ironic erosion. Think of all that cash flow left to bleed a world away. What possessed Tillman who, having everything, desperately needed something? Gray-haired wise men, his former bosses, lobby for open trade while their own children play dress-up with the offspring of hostile foreign interests in Swiss boarding schools, proving that irony is wasted on the powerful.

Seasoned war planners find religion in the media glare. Shock and awe reveals itself as an epiphany launched on a boomerang. Some bunkers, we find, are like old souls, too sublime even for the smartest bombs. Dr. Strangelove, permanently estranged from Aeschylus, denied to the end that smart bombs always double back on their makers. The chorus shouts back: That's a clever bandying-about of the western canon alright, but these people are a mystery with their aversion to late-model cars and stone-washed jeans. How will we buy them off?

Undeterred by the bounty lying just outside their vast network of ill-appointed caves, hungry men hang on as they have against millennia of interlopers. There isn't a Marshall Plan big enough to resolve their endurance. Each surgical strike serves only to drive them further into subterranean wells of contemplation where they map, circle by concentric circle, the contours of Hollywood's darkest fears. How can their access to Dante's air-flight schools make the Homeland any safer? While we face an acute shortage of Arabic translators and porous borders, their devils move back and forth across our cratered cities with an infidel's impunity.

America scrambles for the exits, reserving its applause for a commercial interruption that never seems to arrive. Find for us that style-conscious former Baathist party member who will rise to claim vast sums of unmarked bills while condemning car bombs for their formulaic repetition. We seek a graven image, a poodle in our likeness: a Marcos, a Diem, a Batista; a man who wears his spirit on his sleeve where it dangles like a vetted script.

During this interregnum, dispatches from the front are a déjà vu of prior endings. In an asynchronous conflict, no officer's commission is safe. Careers are destroyed. Mothers nurse tactical advantage. Every baby is a bomb. No, this enemy, engaged at the throat of our advancements, is impervious to suspicious white powders and concluding sunsets. Life is a plot hatched for endless struggle. Denouement is an abomination. Virgins want blood. Irony is a decadent western literary device, the pornographer turned to seedy language when his movies fail to register. The box office can't tally when the credits don't roll.

Meanwhile that overworked *deus ex machina*, Saigon's last-shining-copter-on-a-hill, stands ready to pull the post-Pepsi generation from the roofs of burning theatres. How many times can it be relied upon? Affix a new world order to those evacuating skids and mission creep wins. As our civilization extends its tours-of-distraction, those made rigid stand ready to make short work of it.

Warehouses of sentiment and period dress—narrative arcs safely landed, the warm bosom of resolution—sink in the Ozymandian sands. Prophecy, that contrary bitch, proves once again she has a taste for mighty armies. How would that great completist, Cecil B. DeMille, stanch this burgeoning desert flower, this gratuitous wound of the world that so clearly wants to flow like a salve over every artifice the Duke, consummate actor, once held sacred?

FLAMES OF OUR FATHERS

"The hidden hand of the market will never work without a hidden fist...And the hidden fist that keeps the world safe for Silicon Valley's technologies to flourish is called the U.S. Army, Air Force, Navy and Marine Corps."—Thomas Friedman, "The Lexus and the Olive Tree"

Incautious men have no business heading unchecked superpowers. To quote an operable malapropism, they routinely 'mis-underestimate' their foes. But that's only if there is an abiding interest in avoiding conflagration. Could it be that casual post-war planning in Iraq reflected apathy towards a post-war period at all? There's just so much riding on war these days. One man's battle fatigue is another's gross receipts. *Ka-ching*. In short order, the smoke, like the plot, thickens.

In a bygone age, wars ran their course, thank God. Armies collapsed, nations bankrupted themselves. It was when war bonds, high-tech weaponry and strategic ambivalences bumped the gold standard, human blood and a Hun at the door that perpetual conflict really found its legs. In 1997 with the Cold War in abeyance, America's prospects for an adversary-in-perpetuity lay in ruins. Peace threatened to engulf the world. Indeed the post-Cold War era got hijacked on the way to the armistice by a bunch of guys who couldn't bear to see their war economy fade without a fight. By all rights, we were owed a peace dividend. Instead, a new *causa belli* was being fashioned in the think tanks of Washington. An ominous new group consisting of a by-now familiar roster (Wolfowitz, Rumsfeld, Cheney, Libby, et al.) was hard at work cobbling America's permawar agenda under the masthead of the Project for a New American Century (PNAC). Acquiescing to peace—these sage hawks counseled in the boldest of doublespeak—would be a sure signal of weakness. Perpetual war was the key to holding the peace.

Prominent European intellectual Giorgio Agamben calls this permanent fire drill the *State of Exception*. In his book of the same name, Agamben charges the Bush administration with consciously attempting to transform the post-9ıı state of emergency into a permanent governing principle. When the state of exception is installed, large chunks of the liberal democratic tradition fall away—the better to vanquish a menace of exceptional proportion. Civil rights, legal search and seizure, habeas corpus: all these hard-won traditions are candidates for repeal when the threat is large enough to warrant it.

The menace du jour—terror—is really an existential condition with a capacity for inexhaustible self-renewal. Properly manipulated, terror is the enemy that never goes away. How evil, how brilliant—a Halliburton wet dream as though the doctor himself (Strangelove) ordered it. Here's Agamben in his own words:

"President Bush's decision to refer to himself constantly as the 'Commander in Chief of the Army' after September 11, 2001, must be considered in the context of this presidential claim to sovereign powers in emergency situations. If, as we have seen, the assumption of this title entails a direct reference to the state of exception, then Bush is attempting to produce a situation in which the emergency becomes the rule, and the very distinction between peace and war (and between foreign and civil war) becomes impossible."

Agamben, treading Orwell's *war is peace* conundrum, anticipates exactly the current rhetorical debate being waged over the precise nature of Iraq's conflict (e.g. foreign vs. civil vs. sectarian, etc.) This mischievous blurring of the lines—so crucial to a fascistic subjugation of the truth—lies at the heart of PNAC's 1997 Statement of Principles:

"As the 20th century draws to a close, the United States stands as the world's preeminent power. Having led the West to victory in the Cold War, America faces an opportunity and a challenge… We are in danger of squandering the opportunity and failing the challenge…We seem to have forgotten the essential elements of the Reagan Administration's success: a military that is strong and ready to meet both present and future challenges."

Having led the West to victory…we are in danger. Such nefarious circumlocution. Surely it's true then that war serves none but the military industrial complex as *victory*, the ostensibly preferred outcome, delivers us only to the precipice of fresh peril. We're in the flying bullet business after all. Even Reagan's controversial military build-up could camouflage itself with a seemingly credible and existent threat, the Soviet Union. *Squandering the opportunity?* Here again, we encounter odd rhetoric for a basking victor. The question is begged: a military *strong and ready* to deter whom? Let it be known that when we were owed a ticker tape parade, the real spoils of war amounted to the near-certain prospect of further war. The PNAC inference is as clear as it is dispiriting: a cessation of hostilities is hostile to America's interests, certainly to the economic interests of a certain few *in* America. With obligatory rectitude, the word 'defense' appears four times in the brief preamble. Such a nice Gandhian touch, that.

For those who doubt the strange, veering careers of wars, they might séance the Archduke Ferdinand, that wholly improbable Typhoid Mary of WWI. Next domino? Iran. Certainly Bush, wallowing in Churchillian self-pity, looks ready to enlarge the present conflict. An injured narcissist, he will camouflage his blunders, draw perverse strength from his unpopularity, and roll the dice on the long view of history. What has he got to lose? The generals call it 'failing forward'. Bush is in dire need of WW III to salvage his legacy. Scrupulous flag-watchers will beg to differ as Israel may strike the first blow. But for all practical purposes, where does Israel end and America begin anymore? Kudos to AIPAC for rendering such nation-state exactitudes between Zionist comrades-in-arms all but moot.

If the health of a Republic is measured by the vigor of its principled opposition, then our protector-heroes were notable for their woefully thin ranks. Three renegades distinguished themselves: Senators Robert Byrd, Russ Feingold and Chuck Hagel. For the most part however the system marched headlong into conflagration under the watchful stare of a bunch of corporatist Zionist fire-starters. In sickening, time-honored fashion, the powerful—significantly richer, all limbs intact—will be pulled from burning buildings by common men and women of uncommon courage and valor. That's the way this criminal enterprise operates. Though it's one hell of a fire they've handed us this time.

THE MANIFEST HIJACKING OF DESTINY

On CNN's January 18, 2003 *Capital Gang* program, two months before the start of *Operation Iraqi Freedom*, consummate Washington insider Robert Novak offered up a number of tantalizing off-the-record statements from a high-placed source suggesting a *raison d'etre* for the Iraq War. To my knowledge, none of the current retrospectives has properly delved this line of inquiry.

Here are some excerpts from the transcript (I have italicized the more relevant text):

NOVAK: …the last thing that the hawks inside the administration, and their friends outside the administration, want is a coup d'etat that would replace Saddam Hussein. They want a war as a *manifestation of U.S. power* in the world and as a sign that the United States is capable of changing the balance of power and the political map of the Middle East.

NOVAK: All right. Talking to a senior official, and he said to me, he said, Well, if we don't hit in Iraq, where are we going to hit? And they—it's a desire that the United States, the superpower, is going to *manifest its authority* to the rest of the world.

Manifest—Novak uses the word twice. So we labor today under a manifestation of power and authority gone horribly wrong. The ensuing *cul de sac* is something resembling war. At least, it shares many common traits with war: bullets, tanks, generals, combat deaths. Yet sometimes the apt word eludes. Like our Malapropist-in-Chief,

America seems at a loss, both for precedent and for apropos language. In our loss, we retreat to a venerable term: war.

The implications of Novak's off-the-record comments from a senior administration official hint at the maddeningly elusive smoking gun. In fairness, the smoke is thick. For not only were WMD's a pretext, Saddam Hussein's ouster was a pretext, which is to say regime change was a pretext, which is to say Iraq itself was a pretext. Imagine the Nazis being mere pretexts for WWII. The explosiveness of Novak's inferences cannot be overstated. The question begs on interminably: Why did we go there in the first place?

The whole adventure was to be a bold demonstration of American power, and perhaps, if Novak's source is correct, nothing much more than a devastating and, dare we say, symbolic show of force. The words, many long-discarded, provide the fossil record. 'Shock and awe', pregnant with smug self-certitude, seems to promise Strangelove's bomb of last resort. Later on, we are forced to acknowledge the term's ironic nexus: astonishing naiveté.

War is our default descriptor. The weight of accumulated error and unintended consequence—the storied fog of war—renders it the only word capable of approximating the present calamity. We graduated, both in rhetoric and circumstance, into war. This is mission creep of the worst kind.

Though of larger scale, the prototype for this operation was quite likely George H. W. Bush's *Operation Just Cause* which overthrew Panama's General Manuel Noriega in 1989. No one calls that fifteen-day operation a 'war'. But it might have sprouted bellicose wings had Noriega proven a more resilient opponent.

Seeking to parade the manifest authority and capabilities of Zionist power and prestige, this conflict came saddled with an agenda of ridiculous proportion. Novak's source goes so far as to express trepidation at the prospect of Hussein leaving power before a war can be commenced. After all, how could the neo-con aggression issue forth without the requisite scapegoat? What reason would then be offered to the American people? More important, why is the *real* reason still unmentionable even now?

Indeed this decidedly muscular, preemptory vision of America's strategic role in the post-Cold War world bears the unmistakable imprimatur of Leo Strauss' spiritual benefaction, the *Project for a New American Century (PNAC)*. And well it should. There's every chance Novak's senior official was a PNAC signatory: Cheney, Rumsfeld, Libby, Wolfowitz or Feith.

The obtuse complexion of the 'real' *causi belli*—not to mention callous disregard for the attendant human suffering—betrays a distinctly Straussian tone—the elite vanguard frothing the proles to action through the spinning of visceral exoteric tales. The great WMD chase was a comic book treasure hunt, the indispensable first-order pretext used for getting us over there. Once there, we could be marched in any direction and for whatever purpose.

Despite an avalanche of books, the American people are still not privy to the real story. Perhaps the 'real' reason confirms the worst of the anti-AIPAC charges: that the war was fought largely at the behest of Israel for the purpose of cowing any potential aggressors in the region. This would make America's military essentially a mercenary force, answerable in the first instance to Zionist interests as opposed to strictly American ones. But at this late juncture, who can reasonably suggest that Zionist and American interests are anything but inextricably linked, some might say tragically bound? This extinguishment of peculiar American regional interests may represent the single greatest triumph of Zionism to date; though it comes at a great cost to America's standing among non-Zionist, often oil-rich, entities with whom there might never have been a natural antipathy.

As Heraclitus famously said, the same river is never crossed twice. The war is real today. It cannot be suspended with a muttered apology. Our enemies' passions and hatreds are not rescindable. The war, perhaps a gratuitous misadventure at its inception, is an incontrovertible war now.

Here then is the concomitant peril: Just as the enormity of the judgmental errors—if not the outright malfeasance—of our government dawns on the American people, we have a war that cares little how surreptitiously we were led into it. Wholesale disavowal of the unpalatable is a facet of human nature. At the point of maximum disgust, we are being asked to show maximum resolve, though every fiber of the body politic may wish to recoil from the dastardliness of the initial deception.

Today's relevant question thus may be, can the American people resolve to remain in a war that never needed to be fought but must be finished now? One very real peril is a knee-jerk post-Vietnam revulsion for 'all things war' and fresh calls for a new American isolationism. America's Iraq blunder could swing the pendulum away from war—any war—for a generation or more. Unless of course fresh war can somehow be made to self-perpetuate and public opinion be rendered moot.

Realizing the growing fervor of the American anti-war movement, those with overriding interests in the region are aware of the insurmountable skepticism another WMD dog-and-pony-show would face. Thus the next intended war—with Iran—must appear simply to 'happen' thereby hopping over any deliberative preambles.

The recent deployment of two carrier groups to the Gulf, the apprehension of Iranian diplomatic personnel in Baghdad (an act of war by itself), the suspected kidnapping of Revolutionary Guard officers, any of these could serve as a sort of 'Archduke Ferdinand moment'. Certainly none of these actions are consistent with a newly circumspect government re-evaluating the prudence of short-fuse military intervention. Once the proper fuse is lit, the phenomenon-that-is-war seizes the initiative. Some factions would applaud such a fortuitous accident.

This strategy of obliquely 'teetering' into a war with Iran was lent further credence by real-politiknik Zbigniew Brzezinski in his testimony before The Senate Foreign Relations Committee on February 1. There, he outlined a plausible scenario whereby such an 'accidental war' might come to pass:

> "The plausible scenario for a military collision with Iran involves Iraqi failure to meet the benchmarks, followed by accusations of Iranian responsibility for the failure, then by some provocation in Iraq or a terrorist act in the United States

blamed on Iran, culminating in a, quote, unquote, "defensive" U.S. military action against Iran, that plunges a lonely America into a spreading and deepening quagmire eventually ranging across Iraq, Iran, Afghanistan and Pakistan."

In a recent *New Yorker* piece, '*The Redirection*', Seymour Hersh details the covert activities being coordinated out of the Vice President's office for the purpose of inciting war with Iran. According to Hersh, Cheney is financing covert operations against Iran. The point is we may already be at war with Iran. Who knew?

Then there's this as reported by the Jewish Telegraphic Agency on March 14:

> "AIPAC lobbying helped remove a provision from a bill that would have required President Bush to seek congressional approval for war against Iran. A number of congressional sources confirmed that the American Israel Public Affairs Committee backed dropping the provision from the Iraq war spending bill introduced Tuesday by Democrats. The bill ties funding to deadlines for withdrawal from Iraq. AIPAC and a number of Democrats close to Israel said the provision would have hampered the president as he attempted to leverage Iran into backing down from its alleged nuclear weapon plans. Others said the provision simply reasserted the constitutional role of the U.S. Congress in declaring war that is believed to have been eroded by Bush during the Iraq war."

Sometimes the best remedy for a botched offense is more offense. The generals call it failing forward. To the extent there were myriad deceptions, we the American people, tragically, did not extract them soon enough from our leaders. In the interim, our nation's ill-considered aggression has birthed a new dynamic.

Let's be fair. There is always the possibility that the present gang that can't shoot straight stumbled upon a bona fide threat to western civilization in the guise of Islamo-fascism. Perhaps the post-hysteria of 9/11 propelled us into a war that was inevitable, if not for this generation then for the next. This is not a Pollyanna tract. Islam's hostile intent towards the West is abundantly displayed both in the Q'ran and in the rhetoric of its more radical adherents, the Muslim Brotherhood, al Qaeda, etc.

There is the equal chance that, in an effort to eliminate some bad eggs, we fired into a peaceable crowd, slaughtered innocents, and in the process unleashed a blood-feud with the surviving, previously peaceable crowd. For better or worse, we are the Zionist interlopers. But how many in America understand why they provoke such hatreds? Absent this crucial knowledge, how can an effective war be waged, much less successfully prosecuted?

The 911 attack could have been portrayed as an anomalous act conducted by a handful of disenfranchised young men wed more to nihilistic despair than to Islam. Instead it was elevated—manipulated perhaps—into the opening salvo of a war between civilizations. Was this a conscious inflation? These are historic paths-taken not easily reversed.

Of course two despairing realities can be true at once. We were spectacularly lied to *and* Islamo-fascism is a real threat to western civilization. Frankly we will never know if the enemy we now face predated our hostilities—or simply rose, by necessity, to meet them. If there weren't Islamo-nihilists hell-bent on America's destruction before, few would argue that they don't exist now, and in inestimably larger numbers.

Indeed the legacy of this war may be that it is the precursor to series of follow-on wars, the first confused battle in an inter-civilizational conflict. Gone is the luxury of calling the whole thing off. We have allowed lies and deceptions to govern our nation's actions for too long. Now we are tasked with defeating an enemy perhaps of our own making. The crowning tragedy is that the inevitability of this conflict will never be known. At this stage, the enemy isn't asking either.

CURRENCY OF THE REALM

THE MILL-RACE: OVERPRODUCTION, INTERRUPTED

> In close-ups now, you can see it in every face,
> despite the roped rain light pouring down the bus-windows—
> it's the strain of gravity itself, of life hours cut off and offered
> to the voice that says "Give me this day your
> life, that is LABOR, and I'll give you back
> one day, then another. For mine are the terms."
> —from 'The Mill-Race' by Anne Winters

We have been trained into an-almost Pavlovian aversion to Marx and Engels here in the U.S. Nonetheless they bear a rereading, especially at this critical juncture in economic history. I should preface my interest in this key area of Marxist thought however with the opinion that practicable Marxism, generally, has shared with the Malthusian orientation an overall deficiency in imagination. Undoubtedly, whole new realms of exploitable human endeavor lie ahead (e.g. alternative energy, stem cell research, nano-technology, etc.) As there is much for capitalism to sink its teeth into, present-day excesses should not be over-interpreted (unless of course economic crisis dissembles into ruinous wars or comparable catastrophes, posing threats to the very fabric of civilization. In this case, all bets would be off.)

Full-blown socialism or Marxism is anything but a foregone conclusion. Furthermore Marx, the thinker, has been ill-served by the various programmatic dalliances—Marxist-Leninism, Maoism and the like—that invoke his name more than his complex vision. We would be foolish to discard Marx and Engels out-of-hand as they offer crucial insights deserving of our close attention.

That said, in recent months I have become convinced we are in the grips of classic Marxist overproduction on an unprecedented global scale. Overproduction is the phenomenon caused by capitalism's need to engage in perpetual labor-cost reductions in order to remain competitive. The effects of this downward spiral are ultimately self-destructive as they eliminate the worker's ability to purchase the fruits of his own labor. A society where the vast majority of citizens lack the wherewithal to consume much beyond a subsistence level becomes a plutocracy in a hurry. Who but the working class can furnish the mass consumption essential for capitalism?

Overproduction is the central crisis inherent in capitalism. That is, capitalism effectively destroys its own markets in an orgy of cost reductions, all in an effort to remain 'competitive'. However at some point one must ask, *competitive for whom?* Production stacks up for lack of able buyers (or, stated another way, demand plunges as the ranks of subsistence-level workers grow.) Witness for instance the acres of brand-new automobiles languishing at U.S. ports right now. Even after accounting for the dislocative—and temporary—effects of the current business cycle, these are the fruits of overproduction.

In America wages have been stagnant for thirty years. However due to the timely arrival of an exogenous labor pool, primarily the Chinese, two crucial functions were fulfilled. One, production could be off-shored and then imported back at reduced costs, providing cheap consumer goods to American workers. And two, the profits from selling that production in the U.S. could be re-invested in the U.S., particularly in the latter's credit markets. (To repatriate the profits would have caused appreciation in the producer-nation's currency, thus making Chinese production less competitive than, say, Indian production.) The producer nations were, in true Marxist fashion, chasing the rather dubious honor of lowest-cost producer.

This race to the bottom in mad pursuit of foreign market-share represents a beggar-thy-neighbor variant whose end result is poverty-for-the-many. In effect third-world production became, from the standpoint of its domestic consumer markets, *prima facie* overproduction, as the fruits of production exited the producer-nation on the fastest boat to the West. Frankly, it wouldn't be a stretch to call this phenomenon mercantilism *redux;* neo-colonialism effectively 'out-sourcing' the costly colonialist infrastructure to an in-country ruling elite. For the vast preponderance of the world, what really has changed?

As the developing nations took their place as 'factory-states' with little in the way of domestic consumer markets (and vague promises of prosperity looming in their futures), the capitalist food-chain became segmented across nations in dangerously unstable—and on a long-term basis, politically untenable—ways. This is also why the producer nations are suffering more than the consumer nations at the moment. In an economic slowdown, a nation of factories essentially falls off a cliff; whereas a nation of consumers can reduce or curtail its consumption and, in the short-term at least, muddle through.

The Chinese and others thus served as 'greater fools' for America's various prosperity bubbles, plowing their stateside profits into Fannie Mae and Freddie Mac agency paper and U.S. government debt with duteous abandon. This surfeit of cheap credit (the un-repatriated proceeds resulting from America's consumption of foreign goods) afforded regular Americans access to homes and other durable goods that exceeded their wage-based ability to pay. Whoever said economics was fair? The more America consumed, the more 'captured' funds lay at its disposal to be borrowed. In this way, America managed to make a business of consumption. Then we whiled away the non-productive hours flipping houses back and forth amongst ourselves.

In his recent essay 'Breaking Free from Dollar Hegemony', Chinese economist Henry C. K. Liu implicitly captures the weird artificiality of the overproduction phenomenon in its current internationalist form:

"World trade is now a game in which the US produces fiat dollars of uncertain exchange value and zero intrinsic value, and the rest of the world produces goods and services that fiat dollars can buy at "market prices" quoted in dollars. Such market prices are no longer based on mark-ups over production costs set by socio-economic conditions in the producing countries. Theyced to compensate for the effect of overcapacity in the global economy created by a combination of overinvestment and weak demand due to low wages in every economy."

The overproduction dynamic in the US was masked, and heroically postponed, by cheap credit from foreign credit-providers. Easy credit cushioned stagnant wages. Americans felt they were richer than they were. This allowed American senior management and Wall Street to extract more money from U.S. corporations than was the historical norm, and to keep wages flat without precipitating riots in the streets. Wall Street made huge profits on both sides of the conveyor, originating the debt stateside and then aggregating it for sale to unwitting foreigners.

Alas America's reduced demand for foreign goods as a result of the current recession puts a stake through the heart of this rather one-sided conveyor. Export nations have fewer proceeds to invest in U.S. credit markets. Reduced access to cheap foreign credit prevents the American worker from augmenting his stagnant wages (and turbo-charging his standard of living) on the backs of foreign creditors. An abundance of foreign credit forestalled our rendezvous with near-subsistence. Suddenly a generation of false prosperity is being taken away, and we stand poised to sample the bitter fruits of our stagnancy. Reconciling with our 'unadorned' place in the world will not be easy, nor will it come, one suspects, without social unrest.

For one thing, re-investing in the American industrial base (after a long period of under-investment) includes the grim reality of competing with the world's established low-cost producers. America's standard of living must fall, probably precipitously, as it 'gets to the back of the production line' in many markets where it once held superiority. Perhaps the good news for the world is that ultimately there will be a meeting in the middle; though in a process of this type, there's more fun to be had on the rising end of the equilibrating see-saw.

The accusations of profligacy lodged against the American worker (which seem to emanate suspiciously from Wall Street) ignore one key fact. The American worker merely furnished the crucial demand-side of a Wall Street debt factory. Moreover they were allotted the role of consumer by necessity and design as there was an abundance of lower-cost workers in Asia and the capitalists required a low-paid, debt-subsidized consumer class to complete their less-than-virtuous circle. By far the instigator, and chief beneficiary, of the game was Wall Street with its 'segmentation' and 'securitization' (cynics might call it the divide-and-conquer) of the debt markets.

The current vogue of blaming workers for their 'financial irresponsibility' ignores the orchestrated roguery conducted above their heads. Just as greed at the top of America's corporations crowded out wages at the bottom, Wall Street's pursuit of ever-higher debt levels in the U.S. served to perpetuate their greed overseas. Together, these forces precipitated a historic theft on workers of all nations. Exploitation of even less fortunate Chinese workers served to conceal the predations on American workers. The aftermath is an American worker who is both underpaid and over-leveraged. Third-world workers by contrast are 'merely' underpaid. Here again Marx intuited correctly the essentially internationalist complexion of the working class. Exploitation is impervious to national boundary. Capitalism is an international project.

One thing is certain. The Chinese and others will not reprise the role of fool. These nations are now earnestly developing their own domestic markets. With the looming departure of cheap foreign money, a generational, paradigm-sifting reindustrialization is required to restart meaningful economic activity in the US. This is hardly music to the ears of a nation that got away for decades with bursts of stimulative credit expansion during business cycle contractions. Politicians are similarly accustomed to delivering largesse between two-year election cycles. However after years of accrued malinvestment, nothing meaningful will happen overnight. Expectation-setting in America will need to develop its long game. More than a few politicians will be sacrificed to America's ingrained culture of impatience. When President Obama talks (as he does repeatedly) about 'resuming the flow of credit to get the economy rolling again', he is talking the traditional short game. This is not encouraging.

We return to the seemingly insoluble paradox of blunt-force capitalism: Elevate the exploited masses and your competitiveness gets shot to hell. Exploit them further and your competitive zeal destroys the very demand it seeks to address. In the final analysis excess or—over—production is a euphemism for too-low wages. Only increased wages over a large swathe of the population can sop-up the excess production and create the necessary supply-demand equilibriums.

As Henry Ford intuited with his revolutionary $5-a-day program, the only workable capitalism is one that builds markets *and* automobiles. The third-world needs a champion of Ford's stature and market power to establish a universal wage-floor. Otherwise with the subsistence wage acting as both scourge and grail, perpetual crisis seems assured. Categorical repudiations are often tempting, but rarely fruitful. Capitalism is flawed. So, to my knowledge, is everything else. The practical question becomes, are its flaws 'more fatal' than those of other systems? No easy answer there, comrades.

IT'S OUR MONEY
AND WE'LL LIE IF WE WANT TO

In Washington D.C. especially, the currency of power is perception, whereas public displays of weakness deplete political capital. I will admit then to some astonishment watching, in recent weeks, key U.S. Senators consistently appear on the losing end of skirmishes with Federal Reserve officials. How to explain the recurrent spectacle of Senators offering themselves up to televised scorn before less-than-forthcoming central bankers? Surely this bad kabuki was an attempt on behalf of the political class to feign public outrage towards their benefactors. The conservation of power argument would suggest such glaring divergences are better ironed out in private cloakrooms. Thus the first stage of the riddle involves asking why we, the grubbies and sweaties, were being made privy to this discordance in the first place. There are a number of possible reasons for this as I shall explain.

The particular theatre I'm referring to involved the Chairman of the Federal Reserve Ben Bernanke and, in a prior hearing, his Vice Chairman Donald Kohn steadfastly refusing, before two separate Senate committees, to reveal the AIG counterparties who received TARP funds. For those who still cling to constitutional exactitudes and powdered-wig notions of liberty, TARP is a specialized acronym denoting about $2.2 trillion of The People's money. That's right. Those stymied Senators are us writ-large—sans the gobs of PAC money and free haircuts. Both we and they were being stonewalled by the bankers, pure and simple. Or is it that simple?

Let's not forget that, while many of these Senators serve largely at the pleasure of the bankers, they are obliged to rattle their sabers when populist opprobrium reaches fever pitch. Hey, why get bought and paid for only to be chased out of town on the business-end of a pitchfork? This brings us to the one hitch in an otherwise beautiful thing. Despite Senator Dodd being the proud recipient of a 'VIP-favored' Countrywide mortgage, the top recipient of 2008 campaign contributions from AIG and the husband of a former consultant to an AIG-affiliated business, we can still dump him at the voting booth. Ain't the vestiges of democracy grand?

Of course this doesn't mean the bankers are obliged to humor their dancing bears. Should Dodd and others succumb to populist outrage, there is no shortage of usurpers ready to fill their shoes—and their campaign coffers—with banker largesse. Politicians are like weeds anyway. Don't get me wrong. Dodd has a great silver thatch of senatorial hair. But frankly my dear, the bankers don't give a damn.

In an industry renowned for indecipherable products and complex interrelationships, Dodd's question was anything but arcane. In fact it was downright plaintive, if not even pathetically offered up by the profoundly ineffectual Senate Banking Committee Chairman. I paraphrase here with just a smidgeon of poetic license: Hey guys, now that we've handed you over trillions of dollars in public funds, can you share with us who got it, pretty please with sugar on top?

At a March 5 Senate Banking Committee hearing on the AIG bail-out, points should go to Fed Vice Chairman Kohn for his artful circumlocution. He seemed to take great pains not to trek mud across Senator Dodd's faltering kimono. Yet after Kohn's extended and exceedingly deferential preamble, Dodd is finally reduced to the rhetorical trick of answering his own question: "So the answer from the Fed, despite earlier testimony, is that we will not get the names of these counterparties?" Though Kohn equivocates a bit further, the game's up. With all due respect, go take a hike Mr. Senator, Sir.

By contrast, Chairman Bernanke's exasperation with that always-scrappy Independent from Vermont, Bernie Sanders is palpable, much like a supine cat barely tolerating a kamikaze-fly. This exchange happened in a March 3 Senate Budget Committee hearing. With arched eyebrows, Bernanke's answer to Sander's pointed question "Will you tell us who they are [that got the money]?" Sorry Senator, but that's a no for you too.

In periods of economic turmoil, the machinations of power become decidedly less varnished. Frankly who has the time to rehearse labored decorum, the honorable this's and the honorable that's? The prospects of financial collapse demand that the gloves come off. Right about now, many of us plebes find ourselves grasping what we perhaps already knew, but failed to confront, having been bought off with a generation of ill-gotten prosperity: the Federal Reserve runs the show and has been doing so since its inception in 1913. In essence very little has changed. It's just that in the present moment, the Fed feels it doesn't have the luxury to play dress-up with its titular overseers on Capitol Hill. So it's taken to wearing the pants more overtly.

Since I brought it up, let me say something briefly about the widely-announced-just-around-the-corner financial collapse. To the extent a collapse occurs, and it might, it will arrive at the instigation of the bankers. They will simply decide to cease lending (much as they have), adopt a liquidity-hoarding strategy aimed at rebuilding their balance sheets, and wait for the rainy day to arrive and pass. Actually the cessation of lending will all but ensure a collapse, as without incremental loan activity, the economy is powerless to generate the new revenue required to service the existing debt. Even if this strategy makes sense to the banks, it will be a disaster for the larger economy. That's because standing still is not an option. (Though continuing the Ponzi indefinitely is not an option either. Yikes. Therein lies the looming catastrophe at the heart of the modern economy. The economists may have a more technical name for this. I prefer to call it deep doo-doo.)

Moreover this decision may already have been taken (sinister music.) Notice how the banks were allowed to re-capitalize themselves with *our money*, in the absence of any provisions to lend it back. This rather one-sided affair will allow the banks to leisurely pick through the ashes of a collapsed economy, reacquiring it at distressed prices. Notice also that, given the choice between assisting the borrower class (via debt relief, significant mortgage restructuring, etc.) versus the lender class, Congress chose the latter. (I knew we should have hired Mrs. Dodd.) The Ponzi noose is being prepared to begin its constrictions anew. For our part, we'll recommence the game at dramatically diminished levels.

Almost everything we are told about money and banking isn't true. The Federal Reserve's shell-game begins with the name itself. Not 'federal' at all it is actually a private entity whose non-tradable shares are held by various banks (many of whom are foreign entities). Eager to maintain the illusion of duteous government agency however, the Fed plays the deferential game of congressional oversight. Many will recall how former Chairman Greenspan used to fill the time with murky and ultimately indecipherable Greenspeak. Back then, times were ridiculously good, thanks to a succession of asset bubbles. Thus the atmosphere was largely collegial. Everyone was drinking the same bubbly. Intoxication was ubiquitous.

Today we are in the midst of an existential crisis of financial complexion. In such an environment, no question can be discarded out-of-hand as being too dumb. So it bears asking, whose money is it anyway? Careful how you answer this question boys and girls, as most folks confuse currency, the duly earned stuff jangling around in their pockets—or an arms-length away from jangling in checking or savings accounts—with money. In fact no more than five per cent of the money supply exists as physical currency, and even the hard stuff is but a stalking horse for that most ineffable of pledges, the full faith and credit of the United States (feeling queasy yet?)

The dollar derives its value entirely from government fiat. Indeed since 1971, it is no longer convertible even to a modicum of gold. Thus money, for all intents and purposes, is an apparition. The bankers birth this apparition via computer keystroke. That is to say, they conjure it entirely from the ether. Of course there are capitalization and fractional reserve requirements intended to keep a lid on willy-nilly leveraging. However the banks have done a great job of skirting these through various off-balance sheet and shadow-banking maneuvers. This electronic apparition then redounds through the economy, not unlike a series of ever-diminishing Matryoshka dolls, spurring additional loans and with them, incremental economic activity.

As progenitors of this mythic beast, money, the bankers feel they have the right to take it all away—or redirect it to foreign shores—with impunity. Indeed the latter is exactly what they are doing today; hence the effusive though evasive poppycock in the videos above. For despite it pronouncements, the Fed was not chiefly concerned about the risks of telegraphing troubled institutions, creating further instability in the system and discouraging banks from availing themselves of our money or as Bernanke stated, "[revealing the names] is counterproductive and will destroy the value of the program…banks will not come to the discount window…" Despite its merits as a facile sound-bite, this explanation is disingenuous at best. As Sanders pointed out, having its name splashed all over the papers didn't exactly stop AIG from shoveling billions of public dollars into its pockets. No, the larger concern was the inherent political risk of revealing to the American people the internationalist configuration of the banking system. Power is a zero-sum game. The primacy of an internationalist agenda arrives at the expense of national sovereignty. Slowly, but with great deliberation, the bankers are engineering a coup. But if you don't mind, they'd like to avoid a broad discussion until it is a *fait accompli*. Fair enough?

It should surprise no one then that only a few weeks later, we were to learn that much of 'our' money—ostensibly earmarked for 'American insurer' AIG—went to the latter's foreign counterparties. In fact this might have remained a secret were it not for AIG's decision to release the counterparty list on its own initiative, partly to tamp down the growing outrage over executive bonuses. (At the time of this writing $50 billion went to foreign counterparties, mostly European banks. Legislation that requires further Fed transparency is being considered on Capitol Hill. Perhaps banker arrogance has finally forced the hand of Congress. Only time will tell.)

Predictably, the hue and cry across Main Street's blogosphere took a quaintly populist slant: Why is OUR money going to bail out THEIR banks? The Federal Reserve knew this rather inconvenient truth would precipitate a PR debacle in Peoria. That's why they so valiantly resisted revealing the counter-parties in the first place.

We are thus embroiled in a jurisdictional dispute that gives sudden credence to the traditionally fringe New World Order crowd. Given that the Federal Reserve is little more than the U.S. fiduciary of an international banking cartel, shifting public monies from the U.S. Treasury to, say, Spain's Banco Santander or France's Societe Generale (among others) amounts to a series of left-pocket-right-pocket transactions. That's what *internationalism* means: the world becomes their indiscriminate oyster. To the globetrotting banker set, national borders are mere technicalities, *pro forma* bottlenecks festooned with pesky barbed-wire. Their France is our Indiana. Whereas Middle America still salutes all the requisite homilies—apple pie, America do-or-die, taxation with representation, *semper fidelis*—the banking class has long-since abandoned these nationalist sentimentalities. Without donning a tin-foil hat (or adjudicating on the merits of a transnational perspective) this jurisdictional dispute would seem to comport the New World Order in a nutshell.

The point is this: money belongs to the bankers, to be dispatched to any jurisdiction they please under cover of their ambiguously-arranged 'quasi-public' entities, the central banks. Moreover this flow of funds is largely impervious to domestic oversight. So it's their money—to the extent that it can even be said to exist at all. We only borrow it—both literally and figuratively. Indeed one could argue the most determinative subtext in American history has been the battle for and against a national bank, dating back, with subsequent fits and starts, to Alexander Hamilton's establishment of the First Bank of the United States on the behest of European banking interests. As Jefferson would argue, unrestrained recourse to borrowed money (in a simpler day the sin was usury) comes at great peril to individual liberty, sovereignty, self-determination and all those other niceties that increasingly resemble so many lace doilies in a roped-off tour of Monticello. To the extent you *owe*, you are in part *owned*, as the shared etymology of these words so aptly implies. Cloaking usury in quasi-governmental vestments is tantamount to dedicating the body as a shrine to cancer.

So it's as good as money in the bank is it? Or is that a bankrupt homily ascribing metaphysical certitude where none exists? Main Street America needs to reflect carefully on the very nature and origin of money. For, as the bankers giveth so they taketh away. Feeling richer? I wouldn't bank on it.

WHEN CURRENCY BECOMES A FIAT FOR OXYGEN, ALL BREATHING MUST LEAVE THE ROOM

"This business about appetite for risk or ability to shift risk is all crap."—from The Institutional Risk Analyst: "The Vigorish of OTC: Interview with Martin Mayer"

The Bid is the Father of the Ask

When risk conforms by profile or by sleight
of counter-party hand to prop a shoe
that cannot fall, or engineers a flight
to weaker hands—sound *bid*'s been bid adieu.
When *ask* splits distance value can't divine
from hubris, moral compassing won't span
the gulf. Thus marked to market, we resign
to Fate which underwrites the boldest plan
meting out peril rough to right reward
and meet our Maker on a cropless field,
bankrupted by the grains we sought to hoard
and harvest in totality. Then yield
our epic greed to untransacted glare
undone by Him, black swans and *laissez-faire*.

Something is afoot that, so far, eludes the most sprawling macroeconomic theories. Like the ultimate exogeneity or game-changing black swan, the best evidence of a dawning paradigm is that few things make sense through the old glasses. As T. S. Eliot remarked of great poetry (and I paraphrase), its arrival is felt before its impact is understood. In this instance, we will regret mistaking a lack of understanding for a lack of arrival.

Not surprisingly, all roads lead to modern-day Rome. Indeed there is a super-dimensional aspect to America's most-favored nation status as propagator of the world's reserve currency. When Zimbabwe prints money, hyper-inflation results, the standard textbook stuff. Land reform programs (i.e. taking arable land from those with green thumbs and giving it to those with brown noses) will earn you 11,000,000% inflation.

It's said the rich are different. So is King Dollar. Indeed Mugabe must salivate at American alchemy as Fed Chairman Ben Bernanke's profligacy spurs a 'flight to dollar safety'. It doesn't take a PhD in Economics to glean from the chart below that business as usual has been shattered. Fed panic speaks in the sheer verticality. The recent growth in the US monetary base has been nothing short of parabolic. It seems the Fed has been shooting a fire-hose through a pin-hole—the pin-hole being the banking industry's reluctance to create fresh loan activity from torrents of new money as they preoccupy themselves with rebuilding capital reserves. Basic economics tell us that, while inflation can be postponed, it cannot permanently be repealed. Not with repeated helicopter drops like this. The ghost is in the machine. Now we await its apparation.

But shock of shocks, the dollar is strengthening. Indeed there may be a technical (read: temporary) complexion to the recent dollar run-up. As the world shifts, panic-stricken, from one troubled asset class to the next, each swoon must pass through the dollar tollbooth. Thus we find wholesale panic bullish for the reserve currency. As *Jesse's Café Americain* October 2 blog entry describes, European current demand for dollars is acute but really a short-term artificiality caused by "a currency imbalance [that] increases the cost of euro-dollar swaps".

Thus the last few weeks' event of a strengthening dollar—*vis a vis* practically everything else—only mimics the trend of deflation. As Jesse says elsewhere, in the midst of "a short term liquidity crunch, traders, in this case most likely hedge funds and small speculators, go into panic selling to address margin calls and short term cash obligations." Deflation would require a conscious central bank policy to raise interest rates, not likely. Dollar strength is thus an unsustainable aberration. Inflation is all but assured.

America should take little comfort from its currency's relative strength. However one calibrates the chutes and ladders, the dollar, once proud eagle, has become a pigeon among sparrows. Moreover the diminishment is a global phenomenon. No boat can avert a receding tide. The world's economy will emerge from this debacle economy-sized. Isn't it a bit supercilious then to crow that the highest man clinging to the mast of a sinking ship is in a position of 'relative safety' when the ship, the currency complex, is sinking? So the last man drowns last. Big deal.

Beyond even these technical machinations, there is a ghost in the machinery of the currency complex that betrays a measure of irrationality, a non-quantifiable 'fealty' to dollars. Call it a force of habit. Other apt analogies? The Divine Right of Kings, *Pax Romana*. People are swimming—partly as an act of faith, partly from a half-century of ingrained habit—towards a lifeboat with a fatal leak. What's the alternative, hugging a wave? For those who prefer casting aspersions with their last breath, they might shout, who didn't pack a second lifeboat? Perhaps it's not a lifeboat at all that will save us, but an island—gold. Perhaps there are better, more utilitarian, stores of intrinsic value: cigarettes, nylons and chocolate for example. Own a warehouse of ciggies and you may one day preside over a small mid-western town.

Though wealth can evaporate overnight, belief systems tend to linger beyond their period of efficacy. A belief system that has held sway for the better part of a half-century is bankrupt (literally), and risking hyper-inflation (after perhaps a brief deflationary interlude) as it strives mightily to forestall the inexorable process of its decline. History is littered with denialists. The bitter prospect of marking-to-market is an admission of lost might, a medicine far too hard to swallow. An empire collapses back to more manageable perimeters only with great reluctance. For one thing, retreat precipitates ugly feed-back loops. Other uppity frontier regions become emboldened. The empire buzzes with insurrection. The powers-that-be will embrace denial before they embrace retreat. We are about to learn just how dangerous a wounded Master of the Universe can be.

Jawboning

Depression. That's a word they're loath to say,
the men whose jobs revolve around the myth
that words, like sticks and stones, put trends in play
not easily reversed. They'll take the fifth
before reciting populist accounts
as though hard times held under house arrest
might huddle in the basement. All that counts
is what gets counted—keep the bloody rest.
No gesture pays for braces. No harangue
can cure the blind of pathologic greed.
Econometric models lack the pang
of hunger. How the poor excel at need.
Depression means no money, simply put
—a truth too bare to snare a tailored suit.

One wonders, can the *Pax Americana*/Bretton Woods/Plaza Accord regime truly hand the baton to a new world order (lower case) without a resounding capitulation followed by an ensuing period of collapse? The Visigoths destroyed Rome. Centuries of darkness ensued before *Pax Britannia* re-ordered the world. But take solace, my broadband brethren. In the digital era, the prior business of centuries now concludes itself in mere decades if not years. Computers aren't going away.

How can the world purge itself of dollars when it is awash in them? It pays to remember currencies are comparative, not intrinsic, stores of value. Thus purging oneself of a currency always involves bingeing on another. In an era of dwindling resources and looming peak oil, resource proxies are looking good—gold, oil. The euro might have served nicely as an orderly re-assembly point. But it's hard to imagine the long-term twin collapse of the dollar and the euro meaning anything less than the wholesale collapse of the currency regime. After all who are the pretenders to the currency throne? Certainly not the yen. The Japanese are too insular to host the coin of the realm. The Swiss franc must contend with a banking system whose short-term bank debt equals 1,273% of the Swiss government's national debt. Clearly the gnomes of Zurich have been busy. By contrast, the U.S. looks positively chaste at 43%. (Source: New York Times; *"The World's Banks Could Prove Too Big to Fail—or to Rescue"*; 10/10/08; Floyd Norris.)

Best not to push too hard on that 43% figure though; according to Mr. Mortgage's recent calculations, American banks' so-called Level 2 'mark-to-market' balance sheet value approaches $7.3 trillion. As this number is a creature of Excel spreadsheets, the market-derived value could be anything, more likely significantly less. Mr. Mortgage's doom-laden prognostications have been pretty accurate since at least 2006.

In short, there are no bright beacons in the world. Fiats of all stripes have been done in by hubris. The loss of goodwill and trust in the power of paper—too hard to calibrate in the midst of the crisis—will no doubt be staggering.

As for the Paulson Plan, it's an insult to band-aids everywhere. Apparently, the master plan is that all scorched parties must show up for future treasury auctions and pretend that their bandaged third-degree burns are mere flesh wounds. Isn't that the unspoken *quid pro quo* of the bail-out bill, uninterrupted Ponzi participation by foreign central banks? What dupe continues to show up for a Ponzi scheme after the pyramid's been revealed? The Plan reeks of global central bank fear. They will pretend on one another's behalf to avoid the eradication of their species. Our currencies are their hapless pawns.

Up until very recently, gradualists had held out hope for a long-term dollar-to-euro migration. However, this trail has become washed-out in recent days as the euro proves itself more committee than currency. This is extremely bad news for a world desperately in need of economic bipolarity. One implication of a dollar-saturated world is that safe havens get repealed. Every kitchen sink becomes one-step removed from a dollar. Getting from point A to B requires a dollar. Of course it's easy to parochialize the debate around those damnable dollars. The larger point is that the world is drunk on fiats: currencies, derivatives, stocks, bonds.

Structured finance always had a Faustian ring as it seeks to defy God's laws of gravity and commensurateness. We've been misstating our income and levitating our wealth. The world's elite are loath to face just how poor we—and they—are. For the populist, there may be a silver lining as the rich—by practical necessity financial-asset-bound—have much further to fall than does the little guy. Thus the collapse of paper could have a laudatory distributive effect. No wonder Paulson sped through a $700 billion vacuum hose, affixing it to the coffers of Main Street. In order for the powers-that-be to avoid becoming the powers-that-were, they need *us* to re-capitalize *them*.

Moreover he $700 billion figure is hugely misleading. As the erudite blogger *London Banker* points out in his October 2 entry, $700 million is only the diameter of the spigot—like an income statement, a mere snapshot at any given time: "Whether the final value of the legislation this week is $700 billion or $150 billion is irrelevant as long as the laundering operation can accommodate the throughput, as that number is only a cap on total extensions at any one time."

Meanwhile the Great American Unipole is sick and getting sicker by the day. Absolute power has indeed corrupted absolutely. Iraq is the military facet of the same hubris. America succeeded beyond its wildest dreams, stuffing all gills with crappy Ponzi paper. The only solution available to the purveyors of paper is of course more paper; in short, a recipe for more disaster. Suddenly that industrial base looks like something more than a grimy anachronism. We make nothing, and the world is beginning to take notice.

Even a well-anticipated freight train is unavoidable when you're lashed to the track. The long-term answer must lie outside the fiat currency complex. But this is the Mount Everest of official denial. We will hyper-inflate back to a gold standard. No one in a position of power and authority will take us there. The currency will first be debauched until only a wheelbarrow full of it buys a cup of coffee. For one thing, influence purchased with sacks of gold is too susceptible to detection. Paper is the currency of epic-scale usury and malfeasance.

As it is, the world finds itself (much to its chagrin) divided into two sprawling camps: Americans and Americans-by-proxy (or if you prefer 'foreign bag-holders'). In short, both camps only pretend at being two camps. Together, they will slide, daisy-chained, into the abyss.

Europe's present turmoil marches the world one step closer to this abyss. Brazil and Argentina, God bless them, have announced bilateral trade will be conducted in their home currencies, no longer dollars. Of course they are less dollar-pregnant than Europe or China, economies who are frankly too big to bail—on the dollar. The euro was to be the world's second lifeboat. Hang on to your ciggies folks.

DINING ON THE FUTURE:
AN INWARD-OUT EXPLORATION
OF COSMIC RETRIBUTION, ALIENATION
AND MARKET DYNAMICS

For many years, the stock political rhetoric was that, by indulging in debt-fueled consumption today, we were mortgaging the futures of our children and grandchildren. Invariably we would cluck our tongues before heading off to explore the efficacies of "an interest-only, payment skipping, minimum payment option enabled, negatively amortizing, no-money-down, no documentation, prepayment-penalizing, 3-month LIBOR 40-year adjustable-rate mortgage with a balloon." Actually this beast is a fiction that appeared recently on MSN Money. Hopefully though the point survives.

To use financial jargon sardonically, we discounted future cash-flows too steeply in order to plump up present value. This present value bias was due to an overweighting of the pronouns *me, myself* and *I*. Each of us was eating for three—and I have the obesity trend lines to prove it.

There is a corollary in the mythological record. When Tantalus was discovered serving his dismembered son Pelops to the gods, his punishment was an eternal lesson in need and unmet desire. Every time he reached for the fruit tree just above his head, the wind would sweep the branches out of reach. As he bent to drink from the neck-deep water, the water would recede. There was nothing capricious about the Greeks' meting out of punishment. They had a knack for matching the underlying offense. Thus we should note with gnashing teeth that this particularly cruel fate was reserved for a parent who robbed the rightful patrimony of his son to curry present-day favor with the gods. The current macroeconomic debate has swung decisively in recent weeks to a discussion of just how deep the ensuing recession or depression will be. If one subscribes to the sublime wisdom of Greek mythology, the darker prognostications bear more credence.

I am reminded also of Goya's painting of Saturn, the very portrait of mindless consumption, as he dines on his own child, one of whom it was prophesied, would usurp him. For the offense of cannibalistic infanticide, he languishes in chains even now, in Tartarus beneath our feet.

Alas there are many ways to eat a child. And what better way to gauge a society's moral tenor than to examine the steps it takes safeguarding the welfare of future generations? For us, this is a very timely question as our society's future seems to have suddenly crashed into the present—and with a vengeance.

Watching the current turmoil in financial markets, it is clear to me we are now reaping what we have for so long sown: our profound crisis in *values* is finally reverberating outwards into the metrics of traditional asset *valuations*. The markets are not 'broken' as some have alleged. On the contrary they are flashing a deep-seated, existential crisis. What is a market after all but the expression of the personal writ large in the aggregate? Like a bad horror film where every corridor seems to house a lurking monster, there is no safe harbor—no rest for the wicked a tiresome moralist might say. *Not* stocks, *not* bonds, *not* commodities, *not* real estate. Perhaps the crisis lies not in the stars (or the plummeting charts) but in ourselves. We are speechless for want of value to impart. Like Tantalus, nothing bends to our reach. Like Saturn, the future has finally caught up to us.

In short, the dilemma is moral before it is financial. No vessel will accept our offerings until we ourselves know what it is exactly we wish to decant and why. The various calibrations of what we hold dear will continue to bedevil us until we can say to ourselves with assurance what it is we hold dear. Profound confusion cannot be warehoused. We stalk lightning with a bottle when we attempt to transact fear and loathing between similarly stricken parties.

I've decided Jesus' rage in the temple was not triggered by sanctimony or procedural offense. He knew that commerce was the ultimate substitution effect—for authentic self-listening. Lost souls gravitate toward the false-solidity of material possessions. Denial is the currency of the worldly realm within which the temple is our sole respite—a precious trade-free zone where *gnosis*, inward-out knowledge, can be ushered forth unguardedly. Markets are all about studying the competition. Temples abet the process of knowing thyself.

It is to the starving man alone that Maslow's hierarchy of needs appears for what it is: a daunting edifice. Pitiable bottom-dweller though he may be, his starvation clarifies his vision. As for you and I, well, we need our Internet, we need our MTV and, yes, a little food would be nice too. Sated by a lifetime of relative comfort, we inhabit a flatland fog of indistinction brought on by the fearsome efficiency of that needs-satisfaction (not to mention needs-creation) factory, the thoroughly-modern economy.

But what happens if the modern economy should irrevocably break down? The hierarchic structure of need would reassert with the onset of hunger (or an equally authentic unmet need such as inadequate shelter.) Hunger reestablishes its primacy in short order. Alienation evaporates like a bourgeoisie daydream. My father, in periods of his life, knew hunger. I never have. To my son, a hunger pang is a sure sign something has gone horribly awry. Dinner is late. Am I a good father for barricading him from the sacred murmurs in his stomach? Faced, perhaps for the first time, with choosing between an Internet connection or a re-stocked pantry, our value-system would sharpen in short order. The availability of so many things for so long has dulled us to the exigencies of existence.

Moreover a lifetime of comfort puts us at a tactical disadvantage to those who have negotiated the rigors of deprivation as a normal course. In this way, the poor stand to re-inherit the earth. While our future lot may amount to a lengthy denouement punctuated by denial, anger and finally—for those few who successfully navigate the Eye of the Needle—a rapprochement with the real. Indeed the poor may be on their way to becoming comparatively less poor as a salutary wealth distribution effect ensues. Intrepid blogger London Banker says this:

> "The crash of global financial markets therefore will have a disproportionate effect on the elites, impoverishing them to a far greater extent, although it will be felt throughout society as employment, pensions, investments and public services contract."

Though he may seem, on systematic grounds, a strange bedfellow, I am drawing closer to a Baudrillardian interpretation of the current value-confusion, particularly the interplay between his functional and exchange value processes. Our frenetic interrogation of exchange value mechanisms betrays a functional value crisis. How can we hope to enter a transactional dialogue if no one can explain the functional value of a Credit Default Swap (CDS)?

What's more, our alienation is so complete that we have lost sight of our needs. Or to couch this dilemma in John Kenneth Galbraith's terms (from *The Affluent Society*, 1958), we can no longer differentiate our psychological needs from our physiological ones. It's as though we've been blessed right into a gilded cage of profound incoherence. Columbia philosophy professor Douglas Kellner blogs:

> "...Baudrillard also describes a situation where alienation is so total that it cannot be surpassed because "it is the very structure of market society" (1998: 190). His argument is that in a society where everything is a commodity that can be bought and sold, alienation is total. Indeed, the term "alienation" originally signified "to sale," and in a totally commodified society where everything is a commodity, alienation is ubiquitous. Moreover, Baudrillard posits "the end of transcendence" (a phrase bor-

rowed from Marcuse) where individuals can neither perceive their own true needs or another way of life (1998: 190ff)."

Alienation has become our edifice, God help us. We have arranged our society on the 'foundation' of a $513 trillion derivatives complex. More insubstantial even than sand, this kingdom traverses the ether every second of every day just above our heads. In typical lopsided fashion, the ephemeralities of Wall Street threaten to devour the very real sweat and toil of Main Street.

The word betrays itself. Derivatives are derivations of the thing-itself. When the foundation becomes mortgaged to the clouds, the world has been turned on its head. Hubris has overwhelmed wisdom—for a time. However as the great tragedians showed time and again, hubris never prevails.

SOMETIMES, IT REALLY IS DIFFERENT THIS TIME

> Every excess causes a defect; every defect an excess...There is always some leveling circumstance that puts down the overbearing, the strong, the rich, the fortunate, substantially on the same ground with all others."—from Ralph Waldo Emerson's essay, "Compensation."

Recently on a CNBC interview, Dr. Doom himself, Mark Faber, surmised that, years hence, people will ask whether one was born 'after 2007 or before' with the same auspiciousness accorded 1941 or 1929. Of course 2007 will go down as the beginning of the Great Credit Unwind, once naively thought to be a manageable brush fire confined to the sub-prime U.S. mortgage market. As we are finding, the excess and attendant defect are omnipresent, threatening to overwhelm the system itself. In darker moments I find myself asking, might the defect *be* the system?

Regrettably, I share Faber's sense of portent. And while a fan of President-Elect Obama, I still cling to the curmudgeonly view that Election 2008, for all its symbolic power and change-rhetoric, is fatally tethered to the abysmal state of the world economy circa 2009. It says nothing of the new President's special attributes to note simply that he will find himself diminished like few of his predecessors in recent memory. Such is the reality that a crushing public sector debt brings.

As for the current macroeconomic debate, we may be unwitting hostages to a lexicon and assorted prescriptive remedies that have been overtaken by strange, new realities. Indeed the current dilemma may be 'extra-economic' in complexion; not so much a black swan *event* as an oncoming black swan *epoch*.

That one really smart guy can pound the table, quite credibly, for a deflationary collapse while another really smart guy trumpets high inflation, if not outright hyper-inflation suggests the extremities of Economic's predictive powers may have been reached. Paradox is often evidence of an imminent quantum reversal. Another way of saying this is that the phenomena we observe defy the received wisdom. After all, what is a black swan but the shadow of a white swan cast eerily above the water line, a Jungian manifestation of the shadow-form asserting itself over the visible, consistent with the equilibrating law of compensation?

Until the massive compensatory retrenchment of what economist Michael Hudson has called our 'financialized' economy is completed the future may lie in a gauzy indeterminateness, governed by contrariness where ruled-based Newtonian strings are pushed to no effect. The arrival of such an era should scare the bejesus out of rational people everywhere. Nothing will make sense.

Breathless talk of trillion-dollar GDP's can subscribe one to a false sense of strength and unassailable might. In fact little more than a massively constructed fragility may lie behind these impressive arrays of zeroes. Alas there's nothing impregnable about a trillion dollars. Bernard Madoff's $50 billion dollar Ponzi Scheme evaporated overnight. The U.S. real estate market is slated to lose six of them this year while the world's stock markets have lost a combined thirty in the last year alone (yes, that's trillions;) so much for the comfort of impossibly large numbers. The commercial paper market in the US is close to $1.6 trillion. In recent weeks, that market has seized up. Commercial credit is life itself. If a trucking company can't secure financing for its payroll, the trucker does not deliver the food to the store. The shelves go bare. No commercial paper equals no food supply and, in short order one would imagine, no society. Suddenly the numbers take on a more visceral complexion. Commercial paper is one degree removed from hunger pangs.

As for that esoteric pursuit of actually *growing* food, would it be fair to say ninety per cent of Americans under 35 probably can't *prepare* unprocessed food, let alone grow it? In fact the college rumor-mill has it that apples no longer grow on trees, but are manufactured at Applebee's for inclusion in those tasty Apple Caramel Supremes®.

For those lacking a sweet tooth, I also come bearing empirical data. Suddenly it's not hyperbole to suggest that world trade is in the throes of ceasing to exist (if the Baltic Dry Index, now 92% below its all-time high, can be adjudged a reasonable proxy; by way of context, the Dow 'only' dropped 89% between 1929 and 1932). A few months ago, many felt that depression was too strong a word. What would they say about the near cessation of world trade, an activity that has been transpiring since at least the days of the Phoenicians? Yes, that is rather hyperbolic. But the point survives the rhetorical flourish: Globalization as some wag recently noted, may be the biggest bubble of all. By all indications, it has burst climactically.

Today's screwy econometrics is the symptom of an existential collapse, a profound crisis in value—or is it in values? To be sure, something is slouching towards Bethlehem. So far it's an indiscernible figure hunched beneath the charts. For a time, things went awry alright.

Economics sold its soul to econometrics becoming unmoored from its progenitor, moral philosophy. Politely, we say it 'went quant', departing the human sphere for more abstract realms where disembodied greed basically had the run of the joint. Human responsibility abdicated to the numbers. The bloodless algorithm took charge like a Frankenstein monster. Now something is tugging us—violently it seems—back to a fundamental re-assessment of value. Right now, all asset classes are rejecting our best attempts to invest them with value: not stocks, not bonds, not gold, not real estate. Only the U.S. Dollar—a currency which, since being taken off the gold standard in 1971, is really a proxy for nothing at all, is showing 'strength'. Think of it, nothing is appreciating with a vengeance. The complete befuddlement is a telling clue. Sensing their slipping status quo, the elite respond with flailing counter-measures, heaping billions here and billions there. Will their crazed largesse ever add up to real money? All things are proving stubbornly resistant to value because there's something terribly off-center—perhaps fatally anachronistic—about our notions of value. We've enlisted a stethoscope to assess the pulse of a forest fire. Or are the old Keynesian techniques killing the patient, a form of bleeding vapors from the body politic?

Moreover central banks will not weather this inflection. Before they die however, they will prime the pump madly. Given the specter of profoundly disrupted economic activity, will their inflationary efforts succeed in sparking an ignominious legacy of hyper-inflation? Keen economic minds remain sharply divided over the possibility of inflation in light of mammoth debt deflation. Perhaps it's time for a flight back to mind-numbing basics. A glass of water has an undeniable intrinsic value. In the absence of potable water, its value exceeds that of a gilded mansion. You can't drink luxurious amenities. Folly gets you dust in a drought. So the USD is a knife falling to earth at a lesser rate of velocity than the other knives in the drawer; this is the oft-cited 'race to the bottom'. Thus viewed in exclusion, the USD appears to be defying the laws of gravity, but only in a relative sense. Fiats become meaningless when they are removed from the context of their proxy. In a world that cannot put its finger on intrinsic value with any dead certainty, the whole fiat notion suffers an even more profound identity crisis. How can a derivative retain value when we are at loss to explain what it is derived from?

And yet just as we are suffering this fundamental crisis in value, there is a $513 trillion fiat superstructure hovering above our heads, relic of a prior regime. This rusty scaffold must still be reckoned with as it possesses very real claims on the real. For one thing, the balance sheets of those very same banks we're attempting to bail out are still burdened with the debt era's esoterica. Indeed it can bury the real, especially if we keep feeding the fruits of our real exertions into its infinitely ravenous maw. Perhaps the CERN Collider managed to birth a black hole before being unceremoniously shutting down for repair? If so, a parallel universe could be enjoying the bounty of our evacuating value. I have a name for this movie: *Windfall on Planet*

X. Seriously though, it's a common plaint in investor circles: Where the is all the value going? Blame the scientific community as they just had to go hunting for the God Particle. Something may be striking us back.

We now return you to your regularly scheduled Planet Earth where everyone seems to be ransacking the conventional stores of economic value. However nothing is offering up sustenance. We seem to be in the midst of an Old Testament collapse of hubris and greed on an epic scale. Gordon Gekko *was* the Anti-Christ. Now old-school morality is mounting an ascent from a horribly oversold position. Does anyone recall when greed was bad? Maybe it's about to become bad again.

I am not a religious man in any formal sense. Yet I feel we are about to get religion in a hurry. The doomsayers may finally have it right. There's going to be a lot of gnashing of teeth. We've finally arrived at the stopped clock of dark prognostication where, if economist Eric Janszen is to be believed, no subsequent bubbles will rise up to save us.

METROPOLIS, EZRA POUND, MAMMON AND THE LAW OF TOO-LARGE NUMBERS

"The old world is dying away, and the new world struggles to come forth: now is the time of monsters." —Antonio Gramsci

The nation's leaders are struggling to address an insolvent investment banking system with prescriptive measures that sidestep Main Street's credit needs entirely. Antonio Gramsci's monsters have arrived, it appears, to ransack America through a series of bail-out monstrosities. But look at me Ma, I'm quoting a venerable Marxist in this season of strange bedfellows. George Bush, cowboy capitalist-turned-Christian Socialist, is taking cues from *Un Hombre de Gentes* Hugo Chavez. Intellectual consistency is dead. Long live chaos.

There's little risk of hyperbole when we concede the conceptual carnage wrought by the current avalanche of events is momentous and revolutionary. Few cherished concepts have weathered the onslaught. Alas globalization was a euphemism for stuffing every corner of the global mattress with Ponzi paper. Financial intermediation, far from propagating efficient capital flows to Main Street, crowded out legitimate credit needs, bringing the commercial paper market to a grinding halt. Risk diversified itself alright—right into the shakiest hands—adding yet more stress to a precariously leveraged system. Economic interdependency extinguished safe havens. Greenspan's vaunted wealth creation was little more than asset inflation backfilled with debt. As asset values recede, the debt remains. The Party of Mao is the *de facto* lender of last resort to the US Government just as the latter is embarked on an aggressive nationalization campaign of its nation's banks and mortgage lending institutions. Confused yet?

If you want more evidence of tectonic form-shifting, listen to formally staid bodies such as the Bank for International Settlements (BIS) and the International Monetary Fund (IMF) expound upon looming abysses and financial Armageddons. Bankers are not prone to histrionics unless of course their world has tipped upside-down. Instructing on bank capitalizations and the delicate nature of the fractional reserve system, at least two recent CNBC commentators have made reference to the famous bank run in the film *It's a Wonderful Life*. George Bailey's heroic efforts presaged the Great Depression. Exactly how far are we to take this analogy?

As Hunter S. Thompson once remarked, "when the going gets weird, the weird turn pro." Tin foil hats are suddenly *haute couture*. How delightful though that, for once, the elite's terror exceeds our own. This is because they have far more to lose from (gulp) equitable distribution due to financial collapse. Even during the fat times vast numbers of Americans were one paycheck away from destitution. Quiet desperation has always been built into the project. For now, poverty is loving the company as it stalks some unfamiliar and perfumed quarters while deep shit threatens to engulf us all in a stultifying classless society. Might both Marx's—Karl and Groucho—find room for satisfaction, scratching their beards in bemusement at the long strange tragicomic trip it all turned out to be?

Ronald Reagan's morning in America lasted right on through to dinner time. But the darkness is reassembling over the klieg lights. Fortunately when the real gets surreal, the movies get mojo. Fritz Lang's *Metropolis* can best be described as a myopic dystopia. Richard Gilzean is right to say, "we do not look at Fritz Lang's silent films for any profound social meaning." Besides, wife and screenwriter Thea von Harbou was the programmatic Marxist of the pair. Among many things, *Metropolis* misses the productivity gains of the computer age by a mile. Today's overclass no longer requires thousands of toiling laborers. However the Illuminati wish to pass along a big thanks for the plebian offer of continued toil on their behalf, cinematically at least. So Lang's futurism hasn't rendezvoused seamlessly with the future. We are becoming slaves to Gordon Gekko's Wall Street, not industrialism. Nonetheless his austere German Expressionist vision continues to evoke an angsty and unfocused dread that dovetails nicely with recent macroeconomic events.

To the unalloyed capitalist, when money ceases to exist, his world has, for all intents and purposes, ceased to exist along with it. What the plutocracy means of course is that their beloved fiat-stacked-atop-fiat complex is sliding into a financial asset abyss. Let's be clear. The world of real things is not in danger of being consumed by fire unless of course the resultant social unrest from financial asset meltdown creates real asset destruction (e.g. SUV's burnt in effigy), a plausible though collateral possibility.

Try imagining an *I Am Legend* corollary where the world is denuded, not of real people, but of investments bankers—Lehman Brothers' Dick Fuld and his ilk; a neutron-bombed landscape that leaves real assets standing while vaporizing all paper, computer hard drives and electronic handshakes (credit derivative swaps (CDS) et al.) David Lynch would relish the narrative discontinuities of a moneyless world—*Mulholland Drive* without the wad of dough. Baudrillard might call it a hyper-reality bomb. Suffice to say a world without financial markets exceeds the grasp of most present-day minds.

Thus when you awake the morning-after, your car is still in the driveway, the office buildings behind your house still stand, the power and water lines are all intact. Inquiring financial minds want to know, yes, but what are they worth? George Orwell said "to see what's in front of one's nose needs a constant struggle." Here's a reality that shouldn't require glasses, but often does: Economic value is inherently utilitarian. That is, when the received wisdom on value wanders from utilitarian metrics, markets have strayed into the realm of speculation i.e. tulip country. Ever try eating a put option? Not in the abstract—say as a capital loss—but with ketchup. There are times when every good portfolio should have an ample stock of tuna fish—and an underweighting of collateralized mortgage obligations.

Are the meek on the verge of re-inheriting the earth? Those who kept faith with real things may be onto a windfall. America has an enviable supply of housing stock, real bricks and mortar stuff. One in ten homes built since 2000 is vacant. A financial holocaust? You bet. Shelter for the homeless? Of course, why not—if we can only shutter Countrywide's byzantine loss mitigation department and get to the real business of filling those houses. Given this surfeit of above-ground dwelling space, there's little need for Lang's subterranean sweatshop, unless of course we destroy the atmosphere in which case it'll be the well-heeled who repair underground while the plebes toil away beneath a pitiless sun.

So don't let Ben Bernanke's existential fear infect you. A few field mice notwithstanding, the housing stock is not under siege. It's the financial superstructure (which in fairness allowed brick to be stacked upon superfluous brick in the first place) that's in peril of imminent demise. Soon it will be great to be real again. Soon real will be all we have left.

In an egalitarian world, Warren Buffet, that quirky billionaire who retained his modest suburban home—becomes even less distinguishable from everyone else. This is a populist's—if not a neo-Marxist's—wet dream. The radical curtailment or outright extinction of financial assets would be a tsunamic redistributive event; Rumplestiltskin's gold 'de-alchemizing' back into straw. The bean counters have a name for it: financial de-leveraging. Last year, Satyajit Das, former Wall Street derivatives guru and author of *Traders, Guns and Money* estimated each dollar of real capital supports $20 to $30 of loans. That's a lot of unwinding, not to mention a helluva lot of rich people.

Then there's the not-so-small matter of sheer scale. Ever try stuffing $1 billion under your mattress? Yes the uber-rich have problems we can only dream of. Financial assets are both their lifeblood and their primary means of differentiation. Score one for an emboldened simple life as our class system looks increasingly to be constructed on the thinnest of airs and graces. Lang was right not to clutter the

Metropolis landscape with an overly complex social structure. There have always been two essential camps: those who leverage the sweat of others and the sweaty others themselves.

As for the teeming underclass, does anyone really believe the whole world will accept 100 years of debt peonage to service what was essentially a financial phantom—ephemeral, 'structured finance' instruments heaped beyond any sense of proportion to the world's intrinsic wealth? Try explaining to a French kid in 2100 that he can't have shoes because the decades-old hubris of some erstwhile Masters of the Universe on an entire other continent must be assuaged. Che Guevara could ride this sort of epic inequity with his eyes wide shut. Half the world would have to become enforcers because the rest will surely not submit to decades of servitude to pay off the greed of a tiny few.

When the Rothschilds facilitated the bankrupt royal families of Europe, they were wise enough not to make the debt burdens existentially unattainable. Kings, no less than serfs, need to see some light at the end of the loan. A collapsing derivatives market—estimated in an October 12 *Independent* article at a staggering $516 trillion is analogous to the burst reservoir that engulfs Metropolis' subterranean city. Rising waters are impervious to class distinctions, drowning rich and poor alike. Indeed a number with nine (some say twelve) zeroes may lie beyond the reach even of the most rapacious hyper-inflation. It is a patently absurd figure in any context—ten times the annual GDP of the whole world. Even more absurd is to express this amorphous asset class in fiat currency form since, if it was ever to descend into the realm of transactional currency, it would submerge the most diligent printing press like a thousand year flood. Scientific notation meets high finance—or high farce if you prefer.

Far better to repeal the financial order, re-calibrate the planes, trains and automobiles in some as-yet unknown currency and START OVER. When greed broke bread with computer algorithms, it broke the bank. Now that same greed, leavened in no small measure by fear, bellows from some back room like Seymour in *Little Shop of Horrors*—feed me! Soon the storehouses will be empty like grain poured into an abyss.

The stage seems set for demagogues more than it does mediator figures in the vein of *Metropolis*' Feder. The young men of Wall Street like the young men of Metropolis have become effete and desperately out of touch. It's no small irony that Lang's initial inspiration for the Metropolis skyline was Manhattan. Grassroots global rage will coalesce as the initial panic subsides and people realize just how much they've been done unto. And they've been done unto a lot. During this Gramscian interregnum, various pretenders to the throne will emerge to galvanize billions of pissed-off humans; debt repudiation—or at least a disavowal of Main Street's peonage to credit derivative exposure—offers rich populist terrain. This much seems sure: Some violent re-assertion of the Real from beneath crushing numerical imaginariness will be attempted. Meanwhile the poor old plutocracy, shrinking in numbers every day, will swear the anti-Christ is behind every bid to disavow derived wealth. Were Lang's Mediator to arrive at this particular infection point, he would find the Brain lost in a maze of hubristic computer programs to which neither Brain nor Hands hold the upper hand. The world is buried beneath a Frankensteinian superstructure of electronic handshakes from which there is no certainty modern society will emerge intact. The better film analogy might be Kubrick's HAL 9000—the computer as functional sociopath.

"The crisis," Gramsci wrote, "consists precisely in the fact that the old is dying and the new cannot be born: in this interregnum, morbid phenomena of the most varied kind come to pass." The original Paulson bail-out was a morbid symptom. Master of a Prior Universe, Hank Paulson (Frank Capra's Mr. Potter writ large) is striving mightily to breathe life into a corpse. Denial is the prevailing mindset of the elite. Without levered and derived wealth, their elite status is finished. They will enforce the bail-out with whatever means they have at their disposal.

Nelson Rockefeller would be heartsick at the New World Order's evolving socialist complexion. But this is not the heralded workers' revolt. As it turned out, a proletarian vanguard was hardly necessary. Good thing too, as they collect their soma every Friday night at Blockbuster Video and frankly couldn't seem to care less. Hurray for Hollywood. No, it was capitalism—biting off more of Ezra Pound's *mammon* than it could chew—that destroyed capitalism. The most sublime tragedy is tinged with irony. Wall Street, practicing a bastardized variant of capitalism, may destroy Main Street's more sociable capitalist model. To refute *Wall Street*'s Gekko, greed is the sickness that swims through capitalism, not capitalism itself. The world may end not with a bang or a whimper, to paraphrase a famous Pound disciple, but rather in an orgy of Mammon.

In the aftermath of pathologic greed—prophesied by Ezra Pound—what third way looms on the horizon? It's possible we may muddle through a protracted Gramscian interregnum before a cohesive new system forms in the vacuum. As for *Metropolis*, it ends on a rather treacly note, everyone living blissfully mediated ever after. The same assurance hardly exists for a present-day world of biologic agents, suitcase nukes and recalcitrant greed. Still, one can hope.

Far easier than speculating on what we will get is acknowledging what no longer exists. A traditionally stratified world will not accede peaceably to flatland status even if financial asset collapse all but assures a flatter landscape. So batten the hatches. Lang's atmospheric darkness, if not his journeyman Marxian storyline and climactic gush, fulfills its task well enough as cautionary tale.

DEL SOL PRESS, based out of Washington, D. C., publishes exemplary and edgy fiction, poetry, and nonfiction (mostly contemporary, with the occasional reprint). Founded in 2002, the press sponsors two annual competitions:

THE DEL SOL PRESS POETRY PRIZE is a yearly booklength competition with a January deadline for an unpublished book of poems.

THE ROBERT OLEN BUTLER FICTION PRIZE is awarded for the best short story, published or unpublished. The deadline is in November of each year.

HTTP://WEBDELSOL.COM/DSP

www.ingramcontent.com/pod-product-compliance
Lightning Source LLC
Chambersburg PA
CBHW020636220526
45464CB00001B/171